Make A Fresh Start With God

Unleash the Power of Your Becoming

Dr. Robert Ndonga

APEXX PUBLISHING
Atlanta, Georgia

Make a Fresh Start with God.

Address inquiries to the publisher:

Apexx Publishing LLC
160 Downybrook Lane
Fayetteville GA 30215
(770) 899-3313

Learn more about the author at
www.apexxpublishing.com

ISBN: 978-0-988766808

LCCN: 2013900415

First Printing: January 2013

Edited and composed by
Allwrite Advertising and Publishing

Table of Contents

Preface

I may not know you personally, but there is one thing I know about you for certain: *you have a profound desire to accomplish something of significance with your life*. Many of us have a general sense of purpose, but when it comes to our internal GPS and the peace that comes from submitting our wills to God's will, we tend to get confused.

I also know that life does not always go according to script. In spite of our best efforts, something almost always goes wrong. We all make mistakes. We all fail. We blow it time and again. In fact, there have been probably moments when we felt like Charlie Brown, the protagonist in the comic strip Peanuts, who said, *"Sometimes I lie awake at night, and ask, 'Where have I gone wrong?' Then a voice says, 'This is going to take more than one night.'"*

Do you sometimes wish you could hit the reset button on your life? Now you can!

There are times when everything you trusted comes crashing down on you. In those moments, you feel alone. Even God seems to have abandoned you. At such times, answered prayers of the past seem like ironic coincidences or cruel jokes. You feel like a gambler who, after a string of lucky wins, risks everything on rolling the dice for a seven. Instead, you roll a two and a four, and rather than winning, you lose everything you had gained! Now you are not back where you started. You are worse off; at least, when you started, you had hope. You felt lucky. Now you have lost everything; what you started with and all your lucky wins are all gone. Now you feel abandoned, cursed, and stupid. You regret not quitting while you were still ahead. You regret choices made that should not have been made, you regret not honoring people you should have but didn't, but most importantly, you regret missed opportunities throughout your life.

You are not alone. In fact, you are in very good company. Even the people we consider to have walked close to God had their moments of failure and disillusionment. When you read Psalm 42, for example, you get the sense that the poet, King David, experienced a deep sense of abandonment at some point in his life. This is a man of whom God said, *"I have found in David a man after my own heart."* (1 Samuel

13:13-14) However, the mood in this Psalm does not mirror the emotions of a man who is anywhere close to God's assuring presence. It bespeaks of a man in agony, the agony of abandonment. You can feel ***aspiration*** morphing into ***exasperation*** and eventually to ***desperation*** in this song written almost 3,000 years before the blues, country music, or even Bob Marley's *"No Woman No Cry"* came on the music scene. In this song, David moved from a tender image of thirst to the urgent questions: When? Why? How long?

As the deer longs for flowing streams,
So my soul thirsts for you, O God
My soul thirsts for God,
For the living God
When shall I come and behold the face of God?

(V. 1-2)

As it turns out, David's thirst was mockingly quenched, not with fresh streams of living water, but with the ceaseless flow of his very own tears. One senses a stark contrast between the delayed *presence of comfort* and the *constant lack of fulfillment*. Meanwhile, each pleasant memory of good times only darkened his long night of alienation and pain. The pleasant memories of joining jubilant worshippers in their yearly pilgrimage to Jerusalem, the symbol of worship and God's favor, faded into a distant, haunting memory. In addition to his inward turmoil, people around him were mockingly asking, "Where is your God?" King David's experience is common to all.

Since we have never met, I can only use my imagination to piece together information about you. If you are like most people, you might describe yourself as being spiritual but not necessarily religious. You are seeking meaning and depth in your life, perhaps even longing for a deeper experience with God, but you have concluded that organized religion doesn't help much. Or you might describe yourself as faithfully religious—a lifelong churchgoer, a pastor or priest.

Life may be working beautifully for you, and you are ready to take the next step in your spiritual journey. Yet, again, you may feel like you are on cruise control—just going through the motions. You are keeping up a spiritual front, keeping the religious treadmill spinning, but your heart is dry, thirsty, empty, and just plain tired. You are a little toasted if not fully burnt. Too much guilt, too many shoulda, woulda, couldas, too much pressure to conform, and too much activity without worthwhile outcomes. In short, there is a huge gap between what is and what ought to be, between the ideal and the real. If that is the case, you may wish to discover the deeper purpose of it all, the meaning, the reason you do what you do, and how to live with intent.

Otherwise, you may be rebuilding after a faith collapse, or starting out on your virgin voyage into faith and a spiritual life. Whatever the case, you have no interest in fake spirituality, forced spirituality, hyped up spirituality, or inflated spirituality. You want the real deal. You desire more than a dressed-up Sunday religion.

Even though our clever faith formulas might bring donations, sell books, and give a certain kind of comfort to people from a distance, I would argue that such canned faith does not work well at close range where life is messy, lumpy, ragged, chipped, and torn.[1] Sadly, our

[1]While it may work for a short while, hyped up faith in many cases can be a source of dread and despair. It turns the question "why" into a weapon and blames the person crying in the hospice or grieving at the graveside. "Why didn't you have enough faith?" It heaps unbearable guilt on the person in the psychiatric ward when it asks, "Why can't you just snap out of it, or why can't you pull it together?" Honest pastors who share the same struggles with their congregants cannot wield "why" as a weapon. They cannot shout formulas from pulpit as though they have no idea what goes on the other side of the microphone. Instead, those of us who live on this side of the microphone must wrestle with disorientation together, so together, we may discover the joy and jubilation of reorientation on the other side.

churches, Christian television, and even some books are merely creating religious consumers of religious products that may make us feel good for a while without fundamentally making us good.

> *If you have a false idea of God, the more religious you are, the worse it is for you. It would be better for you to be an atheist.*
>
> *-William Temple*

The critical question is: How do we recapture our sense of purpose? How do we rise above the ordinary, overcome our fears, and conquer the obstacles that keep us from living our big dream?

With unflinching honesty and challenge, *"Make a Fresh Start with God"* cuts to the core of things and liberates readers to fully live the life God meant for them. I am a fellow pilgrim with you in this struggle to maintain your sense of mission and direction life. I hope that, through the following pages, you will discover truths that are vital for engaging in and sustaining a meaningful relationship with God.

Acknowledgements

Where do I begin? I am indebted to far too many people to mention, but I will include these for now.

Thank you to my friend, Frank Kioko who, with bulldog tenacity encouraged me to try my hand at writing. He would not let go of the dream to see my ideas shared with a wider audience through writing. Frank, this is number one, but I have two completed and ready to go to press. Because of you, I have developed an addiction to writing, and who knows where this may lead us? I also want to thank George Opiyo, my eloquent and insightful associate pastor, for nudging me to leave a legacy for all my toil.

What shall I say about Rose Musyoka? Well, you saw greatness in me that I never knew I had. Your kind affirmations and quiet but steady support gave me the courage to rise up and just try. Thank you for your suggestions on the cover design. I also want to thank Eric Mwangi (Shagy) for your encouragement through the process and especially for developing a marketing system for me.

I want to thank my family for bearing with me in those long hours when I isolated myself so I could find the sanctuary to shape the thoughts and ideas penned in this book. You knew not to disturb the gentle dove of the Spirit when I would be seeking inspiration in the quiet hours of the night.

Finally, I want to thank Annette Johnson, my publisher and editor, for her attention to detail and for her daily grind that helped this book come fruition. Your expert managing and copyediting has made this book even stronger.

Introduction

Congratulations! The fact that you picked this book up says a lot about you. It says that no matter where you are in your journey, you are living wide-awake and conscious of the realization that you were created for more. It says that you are not afraid to try and try again. You want the real stuff. Like me, you are tired of spiritual window dressings.

Frankly, there are times I'm ashamed of identifying myself as a Christian. Not necessarily because of the things I have done (even though I have done some rather embarrassing stuff on this side of being born again), but because of what religion has become.

Although a Hindu, Gandhi admired Christ and quoted extensively from the Sermon on the Mount (Matthew 5-7). When missionary E. Stanley Jones met Gandhi, he asked him why he had not converted to Christianity. Gandhi[2] replied, "Oh, I don't reject Christ. It's just that

[2] Gandhi's ethics of non-violence were heavily informed by his understanding of Christ's message of love and peace even toward ones enemies, encapsulated in the beatitudes. (Matthew 5-7)

so many of you Christians are so unlike Christ." He added, "If Christians would really live according to the teachings of the Bible, all of India would be Christian today."

In a similar vein, Friedrick Wilhelm Nietzsche, a German philosopher and a fierce critic of contemporary culture, religion and philosophy, once quipped at the Christians of his day, "For me to believe in your redeemer, you will have to look more redeemed."[3]

Frankly, there is a lot of dirty theology out there, the spiritual counterpart of dirty business and dirty politics. We might call it spiritual pornography—a kind of for-profit exploitation of people's desire to connect with the supernatural. It makes empty promises: instant intimacy, fantasy, private voyeurism, and exaggerated claims of the miraculous. It is religion that promises communion with God without the commitment of surrendering control of your life to Him—a Christ-less form of Christianity, for all practical purposes. Some people seem to develop an addiction to dramatic spiritual experiences. God has been taken hostage by this brand of spirituality, especially in Kenya, the land of my love and pride.

[3] I do not agree with Nietzsche on everything, but he was right on this one. I wonder how severe his criticism would be if he lived in our day when there is so much dirty theology out there and when believers are acting anything but like people of the Way?

Whatever the value of dramatic, miraculous spiritual experiences (to which some people seem more prone than others), my conviction is that what matters most is available to all - *the daily, ordinary spiritual experience.* With or without dramatic experiences, we can all find, cultivate and expand a quiet, sacred space at the center of our lives, a space where we experience a vital connection with the living God. We can all learn to tap into that quiet current stream of sacredness that runs from the Creator through all creation.

Let me be clear, I am not denying the supernatural, the dramatic, and the miraculous experiences of our faith. I have witnessed many miraculous acts of God. I have seen God answer prayer in powerful, dramatics ways that could not be explained any other way. However, personally, I do not like to talk about these experiences. For one, I do not see that pattern in the Bible. Talking about the miraculous has a way of cheapening them. The memory of the experience gets replaced by the memory of telling the story about the experience. Eventually, the experience itself disappears altogether, and pretty soon, the story being told has very little connection to anything that actually happened. As such, believers are left wondering why God seems to do spectacular miracles over there and not here! That is not what we are after in the following pages.

In this book, I want to invite you to enter into an environment of grace, a spiritual zone where, for once, you discover that you are free—free to continue failing if you must, but also free to start over if you will! I know this does not agree well with those who insist on perfection. However, I have made peace with the idea that I should not insist on perfection where God only expects progress. As such, I am no longer expending energy projecting a false image. I am no longer being drained by the constant anxiety of being exposed as a fraud. The previously wasted energy can now be channeled into actually living a better, fuller, and more productive life.

I am convinced that this pretense-free, grace living, strikes a coup de grace on our pretentious patterns of behavior. In it, we are freed from fixating on what we are trying to avoid or escape.

Graceless[4] living in effect says, "Do not think about Nairobi. Or stop thinking about eating pizza." However, inevitably, the harder we try to avoid thinking about Nairobi or pizza, the more we think about it. Here is another way to put it:

[4] Religion can easily turn people off when they perceive it as judgmental and even condemning. In short, to many, religion has the connotation of rejection.

Imagine the tense teenage guy, infused with hormones, thinking, "I made a commitment to follow Christ at the youth camp and I want to be a good Christian. I have to avoid lustful thoughts. I have to avoid thinking of cleavage. I have to block any thoughts of slender legs. I'm done with fixating on waistlines. From now on I will avoid . . ." You know exactly where this commuter train of thought will lead the poor fellow, not to mention the tremendous amount of guilt that follows!

In *"Make a Fresh Start with God,"* I am making a simple proposal: accept God's grace, and avoidance of sin stops being the focus of your life. This will give way to other noble things such as generosity, creativity, fun, learning, building your business--whatever occupies your attention so you can sin less by thinking less about not sinning.

I write also for all those who may have given up on church or those who want to be spiritual without necessarily being religious. I aim to instruct and inspire. It is a journey in which I join you. After many years as an itinerant evangelist, pastor, university professor, and denominational worker, I have found, as more and more Christians are finding, that neither the conservative evangelical (a theological thought in which I grew up), nor the liberal mainline stream (I am finding more and more in common with this bunch) of Christianity fully expresses my own pilgrimage of faith.

> *What occupies your mind and what you think means more than anything else in your life.*
> *Your thought will determine how much you earn, where you live, and what you become in life*
> *John Maxwell*

I need, however, to begin this book with an honest confession. Confession, they say is good for the soul but bad for the reputation. There is a level of discomfort in writing this book coming from the simple fact that even though I identify myself as a progressive thinking Christian, too often, I am a shabby jerk!

As much as I preach about change, I stubbornly remain stuck in my old ways, wishing for more transformation than I have internalized and lived out. However, then I get consolation in knowing that my struggle with progress humanizes me. My failings only humble me and remind me that it is not easy to overcome the inertia of social habit. Our ingrained habits only die ever so slowly. One of the songs I loved to sing as a young Christian was the song, "I keep falling in love with him, over and over again. He gets sweeter and sweeter as the days go by..." However, truth be told, my life experiences are best mirrored by the words of the old Negro spiritual, "It's me, It's me O Lord, Standing in the need of prayer. Not my brother, not my sister, but it's me O Lord, standing in the need of prayer." From this perspective, I can be more accepting to those who struggle with unhealthy habits and addictions. Rather than seeing them as traitors to the Christian faith, I look at them as victims who have been caught in the crossfire in the struggle against our fallen nature.

> ***Though I consider myself a progressive Christian, too often, I am a shabby jerk! As much as I preach about change, I stubbornly remain stuck in my old way . . . indeed it is not easy to overcome the inertia of social habit.***

I can be accepting without necessarily approving unhealthy habits and lifestyles in others. After all, God accepts me unconditionally but does not approve everything I do.

CHAPTER 1

Who Are You Without the Fanfare?

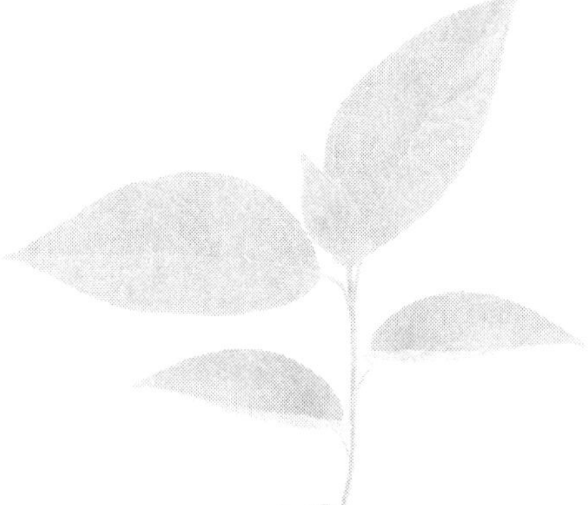

Throughout this book, we will be coming back to this question often. It seems trite and may even irritate some, but think about this question like your GPS. When you enter your destination, the GPS defaults to locating where you are, and then gives you the specifics on how to get to your destination. Before we can begin to live our lives with purpose and intent, we must get real with God and with ourselves. We begin by asking:

- ***Who are you?***
- ***Who are you when no one is watching you?***
- ***Why are you here? In other words, what is your purpose in life?***
- ***What are some traits you like about yourself?***
- ***What are some traits you don't like about yourself?***
- ***If you could change anything about yourself, what would that be?***
- ***What makes you tick, or what motivates you?***

Everyone's life is driven or controlled by something. Some are controlled by guilt, resentment, fear, or familial and social expectations. To a great extent, we are all products of our past, but we don't have to be prisoners of it. God's eternal purpose for your life cannot be thwarted by your past experiences.

Do you believe God designed you for a purpose? I know you do. No matter where I have travelled in the world—whether among hard-charging New York urbanites or humble village dwellers in the deep recesses of Africa—I have yet to meet a person who did not have a dream, a life purpose. They may not be able to describe it; it may be buried deep under the debris of repeated disappointments. They may no longer believe in it. However, it's there.

> *There's an old saying that it's better to try to tame a wild stallion than it is to ride a dead horse. Which are you trying to do? Ride the dead horse of missed opportunities in your past or seize the raw, unshaped opportunities right before you? You belong to your choice!*

You are the only one with a dream like yours, and you have it for a reason. It will draw you toward the life you were born to live and love. God created us to move through life with intention. Even waiting on God is a proactive activity. Even in meditation, we are musing on

God's goodness and enjoying the wonders of his love. Meditation can be compared to a lion lying patiently besides a prey and contemplating how it is going to feed on it. So whether it is quiet reflection or revolution, each day deserves our creative engagement. The Apostle Paul admonishes us that when it is in our power to do good, we should do it; there is far more that lies within our power than we realize. This, in essence is the underlying texture in initiative. In the business world, it is what is called being proactive. This characteristic is described as the "drive to execute." It really matters little what you call it; it only matters if you do it.

Do what? You may ask.

Do something.

I have a confession to make. Most of my life, I was a sideliner, a spectator, of sorts. I was an observer of life rather than a participant in it. You get the idea if you are a sideliner too. For example, in my younger years, at the village night dances, I stood on the sidelines, wishing I were one of those on the dance floor. I had rehearsed the invitation—imagining me walking up to a beautiful girl, gracefully extending my hand to invite her to dance with me. However, add my nickname “bones” to my natural shyness, and you see why, night after night, I could not muster the courage to try it on anyone. With each song, I worked up my courage, and I knew I was almost there by the time the song came to an end. If what happened in my mind had happened in real life, I would have danced a 100 times with 100different beautiful girls. Night after night, I did not have the courage to invite any of the girls to dance with me. As it were, I was still a sideliner.

> *Seizing your divine moment is not simply about opportunity; at the core, it is about essence. It's about the kind of life you live as a result of the person you are becoming.*
>
> *Erwin McManus*

I have a suspicion that there are far more sideliners than we want to admit. There are people who look as if they are on the dance floor, but, upon closer examination, they are really cheering on others. This is certainly true in spirituality. Even the layout of our places of worship betrays us. The pews are set up for observation. A few people do all the work and everyone else watches with occasional affirmations of hallelujahs.

One of the reasons we are unprepared to make a fresh start with God is that we are stuck in the moment behind us. We are afraid to get in the game because we don't want to risk failing again. Sometimes we live vicariously through others; instead of being adventurers, we become hero worshippers. This, I think, in part, explains why we entertain ourselves to death. We find our romance in Facebook (I personally miss excitement I got from AOLs you've got mail) and fight our battles through Robert the Bruce portrayed in William Wallace's "Brave Heart." We admire hard-hitting "defensive ends" in American football, but in real life, we are the ones passively taking the hits. The closest we come to fulfilling our life dreams is in watching others.

"All That You Can't Leave Behind" was U2's 2002 Grammy Award winning album. Positioned right after their hit song *"Beautiful Day"* is a song with the title, *"Stuck in a Moment You Can't Get Out Of."* Placed side by side, the two songs paint a picture of both our opportunity and our dilemma. A beautiful day is out there to be experienced, but you will be tragically unaware of it if you are stuck in a moment you cannot get out of.

Bono and Edge echoed that sentiment in their song:

I never thought you were a fool,
But darling look at you
You gotta stand up straight,
Carry your own weight
These tears are going nowhere, baby
You've got to get yourself together
You got stuck in a moment, and now you can't get out of it
Don't say later will be better
Now you are stuck in a moment
And you can't get out of it.

Then song reaches its crescendo with this conclusion:

And if the night runs over and the day won't last
And if your way should falter along the stony pass
It's just a moment
This time will pass

If you are willing to let go of your past, then you are ready to step into the life God has intended for you. If you are stuck in a moment, turn around and face your future. There is a life that is waiting for you, an opportunity to explore, even a future to create. Time was not created with the power to imprison you to your past. If the Devil keeps reminding you of your past, just remind him of his future. And if the future looks scary, just take it one moment at a time.

Do what you know you should do, and you will know what to do. God gives direction and clarity in the midst of obedience, not beforehand.

If you would have a private moment with the people whose lives you admire, people who seem to live their lives to the fullest, they would probably tell you that they are no different than you and me. It is not about those who have better talents or giftedness or intelligence, it is about moving out of passivity into creative activity. It is about refusing to live your life in neutral, valuing the irreplaceable nature of every moment in your life, and beginning to live with intentionality. Over the last few years, the writings of Rick Warren and Henry Blackaby have had a tremendously positive impact on millions of people around the world. Their insights and emphases were slightly different, but the outcomes were similar. Warren's thesis was a call to discover one's life purpose; while Blackaby's books centered on finding where God was at work and then joining him. Both theses converge at the point where you discover your true self, and then locate yourself in God's eternal purpose for your life.

If the Devil reminds you of your past,

just remind him of his future!

God never promised that we would not have problems and hardship, but He does promise that we can overcome adversity through grace (2 Cor. 12:9). God never promised that we will know everything about the present or future, but He does promise that we can live life to the fullest through faith in His power (Ephesians 3:20-21).

Chapter 2

Redefining Your Identity

With unflinching honesty, Socrates made this bold assessment about life: "The unexamined life is not worth living." He doesn't say that the unexamined life is less than desirable or less meaningful than it could be. Rather, he makes the categorical statement that *the unexamined life is not even worth living.*[5]

> ***The unexamined life is not worth living***
>
> ***Socrates***

Socrates believed, and I concur, that the purpose of life is personal and spiritual development. We are unable to make any real progress in this growth unless we take the time to reflect on our past. Another philosopher, Santayana observed, "He who does not remember the past is condemned to repeat it."

---

[5] Who are you? Who are you when you are alone, when no one is watching? Who are you when you're alone with God? Only you know the answers to these life-defining questions. A part of the journey of self-discovery is God-discovery, because he is the one who fashioned you. There is freedom in knowing who you are and discovering your assignment in life.

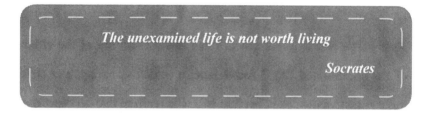

Hidden Mental Software

Examining our lives helps to reveal patterns of behavior that are the core truths of who we are. Deeper reflection yields deeper understanding of the hidden programming, the powerful mental software that runs our lives in the background and away from the visible, observable lifestyles. Unless we become aware of these patterns, much of our life can be chalked up to unconscious repetition.

As a pastor and spiritual guide, I see many examples of the effects of the unexamined life. I recall Jane, a sensitive, caring, and strikingly attractive woman in her late 40's who realized that her repetitive, doomed-from-the-beginning relationships had wasted so much of her precious life that it was now very unlikely that she would manifest the dream of a husband and children of her own. The same was true of Anderson, a deeply caring, hard working man who neglected his wife and children for many years. By the time he came to me for counseling, he was divorced, depressed, and living in a lonely apartment that seemed to mock his industrious past and his real potential.

I listened patiently as Anderson poured out his problems. His million-dollar business was not going well. His vehicles had been repossessed and his home was in foreclosure. The straw that finally broke his back was when his wife decided to leave him for another woman. Only a few weeks before, he and his wife were lively members of my Sunday school class. Now, there he sat, all slumped over in despair and almost suicidal. I did not realize the gravity of his situation until I was alarmed by his last sentence to me. He said, "I have nothing to live for. I have lost all hope."

> ***If there is one truth that is undisputable, it is that while humans have unlimited capacity to mess up, God is abundantly able to save!***

The sad news is that for Jane and Anderson, their faith in God did not seem to help them much in the struggle to get a handle on life. Our society discourages self-awareness with a weekly cycle of working and consuming that keeps us too busy to slow down for self-reflection. *Consumer capitalism's game plan prefers an unaware and marginally dissatisfied populace that tries to fill the void inside with seductive new products.* Thus, to stop and contemplate your life would be a radical act.

The good news is that it is not too late to start over and reap the full rewards of a well-centered life. What a relief to know that we worship a God of second chances! If there is one truth that is undisputable, it is that while humans have unlimited capacity to mess up, God is abundantly able and willing to save!

That Solitary Individual

My journey to discovering who I am in God began in 1986 when I took a class on ethics taught by a saintly professor, Dr. Bernard, who introduced me to the writings of the Danish philosopher ***Søren Aabye Kierkegaard***. I was in one of those ultra conservative seminaries where even the mention of Kierkegaard could earn you the label of a heretic. In those days, conservative talk show host Rush Limbaugh was more popular than some of the professors in the Old Testament Department! So my dear professor secretly introduced me to what turned out to be my greatest liberating theological orientation—a practice of keeping a healthy balance between subjective feelings (emotions) and objective truth (facts). He helped me to begin nurturing the art of critical thinking. Increasingly, I developed the mental fortitude to reject canned answers, even if that meant I had to live with unanswered questions.

In P*urity of Heart is to Will One Thing*, Kierkegaard makes the point that, among other things, Christ saves us from the masses. Kierkegaard believed that the crowd is a sink of cowardice in which individuals are relieved of personal responsibility and will commit acts and hold to beliefs they would never dare to do alone.[6]

When Kierkegaard spoke of *"hiin Enkelte,"* he meant more than we do by our phrase *"that individual."* The closest expression in the English language is *"that solitary individual,"* by which he meant *the individual as separated from the rest, the individual as he would be if he were solitary and alone, face to face with his destiny, with his vocation, as if with the Eternal, or with God Himself, who had singled him out.*

We are who we are in God—nothing more, nothing less, nothing else. This is the center from which true remorse and repentance originates. This is also the center from which greatness springs. Søren warned:

[6] Who is creating you today? Who's been calling the shots in your life? Is it God or culture? Who are you appealing to? Still haven't found yourself? Modern day life is constructed to keep us in the hunt, but we can stop now.

Allow this center in man to remain dulled by the crowd; allow it to continue dissipated by busyness; permit it to go on evading its function by a round of distractions or to lull itself by a carefully chosen rotation of pleasure, abandon it to its attempt to drug, to narcotize suffering and remorse which might reveal to it its true condition; let it wither away the sense of its own vitality by false theories of man's nature, of his place in the social pattern; of its way of salvation. In short, allow any of these well known forms of domestication of man's responsible core as an individual, to continue unchallenged, and you as a thinker and a friend of men have committed the supreme act of treason.[7]

On this note, you may ask yourself: Who am I? How do Ifind my true identity? Until we settle this question, we are still preoccupied with outward arrangements, and the deeper question is still left untouched.

As you think about this question, who or what is influencing your answer? It sounds easy, but it is not. If you had to introduce yourself

[7] Soren Kierkegaard, Translated by Douglas V. Steere. Purity of Heart is to will one thing (Harper and Row Publishers, Grand Rapids, MI 1948), p. 17

(without mentioning what you do) in a hundred words or less, what would you say?

The Performance Trap

We are unsure about who we are because we use people and social structures as our point of reference. We allow others to decide how we view ourselves and then make their perceptions of us our own. Consequently, what we do is measured by others as either acceptable or unacceptable. Driven by our innate desire to please others or at least to be acceptable, we fall into the performance trap, and thus, allow our performance to define us. God, unlike man, loves unconditionally. There is nothing you can do to make Him love you any more than He already loves you. His love is infinite and He loves you infinitely.

First, to get to our true identity, we must isolate ourselves from the crowd and bring ourselves solitary and alone before the Eternal. It was Nietzsche who once said, "In one's friend one shall have one's best enemy." How true! We are our own worst enemies.

To get to the bottom of our identity, we have to pull away the mask. I will not smother you with leniency. On this one, I am prepared to wound in order to heal, to use the knife, so to speak. My function as a spiritual guide is to strip us of our disguises, to compel us to see evasions for what they are, to name blind alleys, to cut off our retreats, to tear down the niggardly roofs we continue to build over our precious sun-dials, to isolate us from the masses, to force self-examination, and to bring us before God—not as we wish we were, but as we truly are.

Our existence on Earth, the world insists, is a mere passing point, a moment in the cosmic process and thus gains significance only as we are identified with a set of external arrangements—as a member of a tribe, a race, a class, or even a denomination. This, I suggest, is the height of blasphemy. The most important thing for us as individuals is to stand as we are before God without trying to wrench away from our failures. Adam and Eve tried to cover their nakedness with leaves from trees God had placed in the Garden of Eden. It didn't work for them. It won't work for us. Remember who you are before God.

Second, we discover our identity by seeing ourselves as God sees us. In God's eyes, all believers are saints. The Greek word *hagioi,*[8] usu-

[8] It is important here to note that this word "hagioi" never appears in the singular in the New Testament. Thus, the Christian Life can only be fully expressed in the community of other believers. We are individuals in community with others. Together, we form the body of Christ.

ally translated saints, can easily mislead us with our idea of saints as people who are far advanced in the life of holiness. In New Testament usage, "saints" are simply Christians—living members of Christ and hence, partakers of His grace and His divine nature. Saints are not perfect, but rather they are partakers of His grace, which sanctifies them day by day.

You may say, "I don't feel holy, righteous, good, glorious, powerful or wealthy. In fact, I am not always good. I do some pretty ugly stuff. I'm selfish," you add, "and sometimes, I know what I'm doing is wrong, but I still go ahead and do it anyway."

There is nothing you can do to make God love you any more than he already loves you. His love is infinite. He loves you infinitely.

Life is not about how we feel about ourselves, but how God feels about us. We must overcome this negative spiritual imprinting and re-orient ourselves with our true identity. We are in Christ. That means God sees us through Christ's righteousness. Simply choose to believe what God says about you.

CHAPTER 3

The Starting Point

At the risk of oversimplification, let me state the obvious: a fresh start[9] with God must begin with an initial moment of awakening, at the point of awareness of God's presence. This awakening is what moves you from the realm of religiosity to spirituality. It is our "burning bush" experience, similar to the one Moses had. Brian McLaren, author, speaker, social activist, and elder statesman of the emergent church movement, makes a compelling case for such a starting point. He wrote:

> *[Some people] think that a spiritual quest of any kind is a colossal waste of time. For them, the only things that are real are those that can be proven and measured. Life boils down to earning and buying and selling . . . eating and drinking and having fun . . . respiration, digestion, elimination, ovulation, ejaculation, gestation, reproduction, antiquation, expiration. Why search for something that we can't prove?*

---

[9] Trapped by harmful habits, behaviors, and attitudes, we struggle to become the person God has created us to be. It is never too late to get a fresh start on life. It is not about trying harder, it's about plugging into God's transforming power and submitting your entire life to him. Age doesn't matter; fresh starts are for everyone. You can begin your journey today.

Why don't we just get real and get over it? Why waste energy over spiritual questions? There's nothing more to life than chemistry and electricity, which is nothing more than physics, which boils down to mathematics. That's all there is.[10]

> *The Infinite! No other question has ever moved so profoundly the mind of man*
>
> *David Hielbert*

Others think that this kind of quest is a waste of time because they have all the answers. They think they have Jesus and religion all figured out, reducing it to their own doctrine or church dogma. *They may say something like this: "It's based on these seven concepts" or "those four spiritual laws" or "this simple five part formula – no more complicated than an elementary equation, really. It's 5+3=8. It's 10-2=8. It's 15-7=8. It's -8+8=0." They argue, "Why is Dr. Ndonga complicating things? Why does he not just repeat these simple formulas and get on with the program?"*

---

[10] McLaren, Brian D. The Secret Message of Jesus: Uncovering the Truth That Can Change Everything (W Publishing Group 2006), p. 4

Being Present

The right place to start is at that initial awakening—the realization that God is here with you now! This means being present at this very moment. Being present can actually be much tougher than we think. I recall many times in grade school when the teacher was calling roll and I didn't hear my name until a classmate poked me on the side and told me, "Say present!" Or there were the times when someone would come to see me in my office and, after expressing their issues to me and realized I wasn't in the moment. They would say, "You're not listening, are you?"

> ***You will find stability at the moment when you discover that God is everywhere, that you do not need to seek God elsewhere, that God is here, and if you do not find God here, it is useless to go and search God elsewhere, because it is not God who is absent from us, it is we who are absent from God . . .***

We are always tempted to be partially here, to pretend we are not where we are, who we are. We are tempted to shift our identity into a state of emotional and spiritual hype, some other kind of "not here" in which to encounter God.

You may have been to meetings where someone is asked to lead in prayer, and then comes this strange, pretentious voice you do not recognize. The guy was just talking normally around the table until he was asked to pray. He then puts on a religious show, contorting his face and disguising his voice to talk to God. God, who knows our heart no matter how much we pretend, must feel sorry for us when we act in this manner. Can you imagine your children coming to you and contorting their face and changing their voice to ask you for lunch money?

"Here" is the simple word that locates us in the moment, the word by which we show up. That is how we respond to the calling of our name. With this simple word, we acknowledge where we are. Desirable or undesirable, pleasant or unpleasant, we declare ourselves to be present to God's presence. Through it, we come out of hiding. Through it, we show up.

Here I am in this point in history, living in today's political and economic storms, within the unfolding drama of human civilization, caught in the integrating and disintegrating forces of globalization. Here I am in my own unfolding story, as a child, a teenager, an adult, a senior citizen, an immigrant. Here I am in this predicament, facing this personal financial meltdown. Here I am with all my problems and mess ups, all my embarrassment and mistakes. Here I am in the middle of this divorce, writing this book, recovering from this break up, picking up my pieces after this foreclosure. I do not have to be someone else or somewhere else—right here is just fine. In fact, it is the only place I can begin my new journey with God.

Finding Stability

The words of Metropolitan Anthony Bloom, quoted in McLaren's book *"Naked Spirituality"*, are instructive. He wrote:

> *"You will find stability at the moment when you discover that God is everywhere, that you do not need to seek God elsewhere, that God is here, and if you do not find God here, it is useless to go and search God elsewhere, because it is not God who is absent from us, it is we who are absent from God . . . this is important because it is only at the moment*

you recognize this that you can truly find the fullness of the kingdom of God in all its richness within you.[11]

God wants to meet you where you are. You may be spiritually wounded. You may be disappointed with God altogether, feeling that He has somehow abandoned you. You may have started out with big ideas for God and have fallen flat on your face. It is possible that you have come to the point in your life where even the mention of "God" is problematic for you. You are secretly so sick and tired of hearing God's name evoked and misused that you would rather not add to the noise. Personally, you would rather speak of God as seldom and as softly as you possibly can.

You may be rebuilding after a faith collapse—the result of a tragic loss, a nasty breakup of the relationship you were so sure was God-ordained but now has left you clutching on to painful memories. Either way, you have no interest in fake spirituality, hyped up spirituality, superficial faith, and inflated religiosity. You want to pull back the mask of pretense and get down to naked reality.

---

[11] Metropolitan Anthony Boom, in Brian McLaren: Naked Spirituality: A Life with God in 12 Simple Words (Harper Collins, New York 2011), p. 31

If this is the case, you will probably agree with Father Richard Rohr when he says:

> *"The goal of all spirituality is to lead the 'naked person' to stand truthfully before the naked God. The important thing is that we stand naked before God; in other words, that we come to Him without title, merit, shame, or even demerit. All we can offer to God is who we really are, which to all of us never seems like enough. I am sure this is the way true lovers feel."*[12]

It's amazing how much can be done if we are always doing.

This kind of honesty begins the transformation process of a religious life into a truly spiritual life—a life with God—not later and elsewhere but here and now. How much richer, higher, wider, and deeper our lives would become if we awaken to the presence of the real, wild, mysterious, living God, who is bigger than our tame concept of God? When I present myself to God, He presents Himself to me. We begin

[12] Rohr, Richard. Falling Upward: A Spirituality for Two Halves of Life (San Francisco: Jossey-Bass, 2011), p. 8

to live with a perpetual sense of here I am, and here you are, in our hearts, inviting constant, vital connection, unbroken communion, life-long friendship with God—starting right here, starting right now. I think that is what the Prophet Isaiah meant when he wrote, "Seek me and you will find me when you search me with all your heart."

All that is required for this journey to start is a little spark of faith—the faith that God is here and that He is on your side. Creating the life you long for involves doing something instead of taking the easy route of doing nothing. The Bible tells us that "lazy men are soon poor; hard workers get rich...Lazy people want much but get little, while the diligent are prospering" (Proverbs 10:4; 13:4, TLB). Human life is built on seizing the hour given to us, and whether or not the moment is seized becomes all-determining. It's amazing how much can be done if we are always doing! In all you do, however, bring yourself to be in the moment.

The solution to your life is to stop running and hiding from God and to listen once again to His voice. Because wherever you are, God will find you. This is not a threat. This is a promise. You can claim all the promises you want to about what God will do through His people, but you will never experience those promises until you act on them.

You may be tempted to let your mind drift from the here and now to somewhere else and at another time. However, resist that temptation and hold the space for the here and now. Affirm that to be here with God is really to be at home, wherever you are. That space, or that home, is simultaneously your soul (*your space where God is welcome*) and heaven (*God's space where you are welcome*).

> *How much happier you would be, how much more of you there would be if the hammer of God could smash your small cosmos.*
>
> *G.K. Chesterton*

From that simple, quiet beginning, see what happens. See what unfolds. Be willing to give up your small ambitions and open up yourself to the possibility that God may smash your small cosmos in order to release your life to greater possibilities. This is the beginning of starting over with God.

Please do not keep reading just so you can say, "I read another book." First, practice here. With God. Now.

CHAPTER 4

The Exchanged Life

Despite having received such a wonderful gift of new life from God, far too many Christians fail to thrive in the new realities of God's forgiveness and grace. Once we are in Christ, our penalty for sin is not only pardoned, but we are also viewed by The Righteous Judge as being completely free of any wrongdoing. And then, amazingly, we are released to a place even better than anything we ever could have achieved on our own merit. We are invited to live by the same grace that saved us!

At the cross, the great exchange that results from the death of the perfect sacrifice is a twofold substitution: the charging of the believer's sin to Christ, results in God's forgiveness, and the imputing of Christ's righteousness to the believer, results in his justification. This exchange takes place at the moment of the person's regeneration and continues throughout his life. It is the greatest gift one could ever receive. This sounds easy, but the truth is that many believers needlessly struggle through life without applying Christ's finished work on the cross.

Hudson Taylor was a missionary to China and the founder of the China Inland Mission. The movement he founded became the prototype of other missionary movements that oversaw the spread of Christianity to the interior parts of Africa. The Sudan Interior Mission and the Africa Inland Mission, which is connected to the Africa Inland Church, are such examples.

There is more, so much more to life and God invites us to drink more deeply from the well of living water available in the Christian faith, which promises to satisfy the deepest thirst in all of us, a thirst that is part of our very nature as human beings.

Early in his career, Taylor struggled with a lack of spiritual power, but all that changed once he discovered the principle of the Exchanged Life. Taylor learned to draw upon the vast spiritual wealth of Christ for every need, and this became for him a great source of inward joy and power. His biographers describe the effect of the exchanged life upon him:

> *Whenever he spoke in meetings after that, a new power seemed to flow from him, and in the practical things of life,*

a new peace possessed him. Troubles did not worry him as before. He cast everything on God in a new way, and gave more time to prayer.

In this rather lengthy excerpt, Hudson Taylor describes his inner struggles:

I prayed, agonized, fasted, strove, made resolutions, read the Word more diligently, sought more time for meditation--but all without avail. Every day, almost every hour, the consciousness of sin oppressed me. I knew that if only I could abide in Christ, all would be well, but I could not. I would begin the day with prayer, determined not to take my eye off Him for a moment, but pressure or duties, sometimes very trying, and constant interruptions apt to be so wearing, caused me to forget Him. Then one's nerves get so fretted in this climate that temptations to irritability, bad thoughts and sometimes unkind words are all the more difficult to control. Each day brought its register of sin and failure, of lack of power. The will was indeed "present with me," but how to perform I found not. Then came the questions, is there no rescue? Must it be thus to the end--constant conflict, and too often defeat? Instead of growing stronger, I seemed to be getting weaker and to have less power against sin; and no longer, for faith and even hope were getting low. I hated myself. I hated my sin, yet gained no strength against it. I felt I was a child of God. His Spirit in my heart would cry, in spite of all, "Abba, Father." But to rise to my privileges as a child, I was utterly powerless.

When Taylor's agony was at its height, a sentence in a letter from a friend named McCarthy was used by God to remove the scales from his eyes, and the Spirit of God revealed to him the truth of our oneness with Jesus as he had never known it before. As he read, everything came together. Quoting from Hebrews 13:5, the friend wrote, "If we believe not, he abides faithful." And with those simple words, simple as almost to baffle description, God made Hudson a new man.

> *If any person is in Christ, he is a new creation, old things have passed away, all things have become new*
>
> *1 Cor. 5:17*

What role, you may still ask, do we play in this journey of transformation? The answer is simply this: be willing. The Christian life is totally by grace from start to finish. God initiated it, God fulfills it, and God will complete it. There is only one who can live the Christian life—Christ himself. He can live perfectly, a life acceptable to the Father. When the Son takes up residence in us, His purpose is the same as it was during His life in the flesh—to do the will of the Father.

Our willingness is expressed as complete trust. Our availability and trust releases God's ability. We trust him to do all things through us. The old cliché is still true: God does not need our ability; He needs our availability. This is the idea expressed in Apostle Paul's words:

> *"I was put to death on the cross with Christ, and I do not live anymore—it is Christ who lives in me. I still live in my body, but I live by faith in the Son of God who loved me and gave himself to save me. By saying these things I am not going against God's grace. Just the opposite, if the law could make us right with God, then Christ's death would be useless."*
>
> (Galatians 2:20, New Century Version)

Dying to self does not mean passivity. Rather, it means when you are united with Christ in his death, you also share in His life. In this, you receive God's kiss of peace and become a part of the community of faith. You begin to live a life hidden in Christ. Three words capture the dynamic meaning of crucifixion with Christ: *pardon, power,* and *partnership.*[13]

Being crucified with Christ brings *pardon*. This pardon means not only forgiveness from past sin and freedom from the law, but also a passionate urge never to sin again (Rom. 4:24–25; 2 Cor. 5:14–15; Col. 2:12–15, 20, 3:1–4).

Being crucified with Christ brings power. This power comes as we surrender to the lordship of Christ. We yield ourselves fully to Him. Our "I will" becomes dominated by "the mind of Christ," and our desires become His desires. We do not live out of our own resources, but Christ lives in us. His power sustains us. In Christ, we enter a new realm, a new kingdom. He supplies us daily with power once we give ourselves to the lordship of Jesus.

---

[13] Dunnam, Maxie D. ; Ogilvie, Lloyd J.: The Preacher's Commentary Series, Volume 31 : Galatians / Ephesians / Philippians / Colossians / Philemon. Nashville, Tennessee : Thomas Nelson Inc, 1982 (The Preacher's Commentary Series 31), p. 46

Being crucified with Christ also means partnership. This partnership brings power of the sort we have just discussed, but it also brings suffering and, thus, another kind of power (see: Phil. 3:10, Rom. 8:17; Col. 1:24–25). Once crucified with Christ, we enter into His creative suffering to "complete what remains of Christ's affliction" for the sake of His body—the church. The cycle of death and resurrection is the rhythm of the Christian life.

In Christ, God has made us who we are now, and we have absolutely nothing of which to boast. It is all of God and none of us. By His own creative imagination, mind, and power, God brought the final person into being; so by the redemptive work of Christ, God makes new persons now.

Salvation means much more than the repair of the ravages and ruptures resulting from humanity's fall. It is not limited to the restoration of Eden's innocence; it is much more. It is the creation of a new humanity and a new world, which previously existed only in the mind and purpose of God. This is "His workmanship, created in Christ Jesus." This new life does not result from a person's good works; good works are possible and indeed will flow out of the new life that has come through God's grace.

With this understanding, Paul's affirmation makes sense and is the call for us: *"The life I now live in the flesh, I live by faith in the Son of God, who loved me and gave Himself for me."* (Galatians 2:20)

Chapter 5

Broken Dreams

It is ironic that greatness is formed in the crucible of brokenness. After a loss or failure, we fight inside ourselves with our inability to change what has happened. Yet, when a broken heart heals, it actually comes back much stronger.

God's light radiates through the crevices of our brokenness to bring hope to a shattered world. Our society does little to help us grasp this truth. In our day, we find it much easier to replace a broken item than to repair it. If it breaks, throw it away and just get a better, newer one. Not with God. He specializes in mending broken lives. He loves broken people, for they are the only kind we have on planet earth!

> *After a loss or failure, we fight inside ourselves with our inability to change what has happened. Yet when a broken life heals, it actually comes back stronger, much stronger.*

Take Moses, for example, in the burning bush experience. Moses had been on the run since his failed attempt to free his people from Egyptian slavery. In his efforts at liberation, he ended up killing somebody and burying him in shallow sand. Afraid his crime would be discovered, he ran for his life.

Strange Fire

Fast forward 40 years. By this time, Moses had settled on the mediocre job of tending Jethro's, his father-in-law's, sheep. It was not the job he wanted, but as fate would have it, it was the only job available to him. He didn't like it, but he felt secure. He was in good company with sheep. At least they would not reveal his secret past.

One day Moses was taking care of Jethro's flock.[14] As recorded in Exodus 3:1-4, when Moses led the flock to the west side of the desert, he came to Sinai, the mountain of God. There the angel of the LORD appeared to him in flames coming out of a bush. Moses saw that the bush was on fire, but it was not burning up. So he said, "I will go closer to this strange thing. How can a bush continue burning without

[14] At this time, nothing exciting is going on for Moses. What he is doing is matter-of-fact daily work. Look at verse one: "Now Moses was tending the flock of Jethro his father-in-law, the priest of Midian. And he led the flock to the back of the desert, and came to Horeb, the mountain of God." He was just doing his work—nothing out of the ordinary—when God appeared. God appeared in the ordinary in Pagan country. Even here God has his mountain-Horeb, the mountain of God!

burning up?" When the LORD saw Moses was coming to look at the bush, God called to him from the bush, *"Moses, Moses!"*

Moses said, *"Here I am."*

We can only wonder what must have been going through his mind. He had 40 years to reflect on his unbelievable life—floating in the Nile as a baby, the improbable rescue by Pharaoh's daughter, the gusty move by his sister to arrange for his mother to be his maid in the palace, the burning desire to free his people from Egyptian slavery. And now this!

Doing the Best Where You Are

We often struggle to find lasting success, a dream that won't seem futile when it comes true. Too late in life, we realize that success is overrated, however. We certainly need to pass exams, complete tasks with excellence, and move up the social ladder with distinction. Along with success, though, we long for significance. As Pharaoh's son, Moses had success on his resume, but its significance at this point in the story was zero. Life had reduced him to leading sheep all day for 40 years. No wonder his communication skills were not well developed. After all, how much eloquence do you need to give a few commands to sheep anyway?

> *History is full of momentous trifles—ordinary events infused with extraordinary meaning.*

Moses, the man who had left the comfort of the palace to stand up for his people, now found himself in the backside of the nation—dull-minded, dead-spirited, and unimaginative. He had all but lost touch with reality. Moses' favorite slogan, I imagine, must have been, *"A man has gotta' do what a man has gotta' do."* Or perhaps, it was, *"It is what it is."* Maybe, just maybe, you and I are a lot like Moses, living among the ordinary when there are miracles leaning against lampposts right on our own corners.

Edmund Burke, an 18th century political philosopher, coined a marvelous phrase to express a solid truth: "History," he said, "is full of momentous trifles." Isn't that a marvelous insight? "Momentous trifles"— ordinary events infused with extraordinary meaning. You have to admire Moses. He is alert. He is present. He doesn't like what he is doing, but he stays engaged.

There's a beautiful, moving commentary on Moses' life in Midian expressed in the names that he gave his children. The Hebrews gave names with very specific meanings to their children. Moses called his first child Gershom, which means "a stranger." Moses gave him that name because he had been "a stranger in a foreign land."

Moses named the second child Eliezer, meaning "God is help," because "the God of my father was my help" (Ex. 18:4). The depression and loneliness of being a "stranger, an immigrant, undocumented alien" had somewhat lifted in the birth of a second son. He had found a way to live by faith in that place of sojourn, in that dull, out of the way Midian, far from the excitement and glamour of palace life of Egypt.

There are miracles where we have been seeing bushes - or whatever matter-of-fact, routine part of our lives we have.

What is the lesson? Be faithful to God where you are. Embrace this simple truth as Moses did, "My God is my help," and God will come. He will probably come when you least expect Him, for God often operates in the ordinary.

You can't plot the workings of God on a computer or organize them in your day planner. The walk of faith is to live in the tension that comes from the experience of the immanent God, the God who is with us now, as Jesus pictured Him -- Abba, Father -- and the experience of the mystery of a transcendent God, the Holy other who says, "My ways are higher than your ways, and my thoughts than your thoughts" (Isaiah 55:9).[15]

Recognize God in the Ordinary

Moses discovered all this not in a church or a religious meeting, but in a pedestrian setting—out in the pasture where he was keeping the sheep of his father-in-law. That's a big part of the meaning of the story of the burning bush: *miracles can occur where we have commonly seen bushes*—or whatever matter-of-fact, routine part of our lives we have resigned ourselves to.

Author Richard Foster once made this insightful observation:

> *"The only place where God can bless you is right where*

[15] God's thoughts and His ways are simply not human thoughts and ways raised to the divine level. Or, we might say, the supernatural is not just an extension of the natural. There is a distinct break between the thoughts and ways of God and human beings. He thinks as we cannot think, and He acts in ways that we cannot act.

you are because that is the only place you are...God had to tell Moses to take off his shoes. He did not know it was holy ground. If we can come to just understand that where we are is holy ground and it is there that we build a history with God and learn to walk confidently with God."[16]

Similarly, you may not like the job you have right now, but use it as a stepping stone to the career of your dreams. If Moses could not be trusted with keeping watch over sheep, how could he be trusted with leading three million trying Jews? Why should God give you more revelation if you have not already obeyed what He has told you?

God has to get our attention before He can present Himself to us. Moses went walking down an old, familiar path. He had probably been there hundreds of times. However, this time, somehow, he lifted his eyes, and he saw a rather strange sight on the mountainside. He saw a bush that seemed to be on fire. He watched it, expecting it to crumble into gray ashes. To his amazement, it burned on. That got Moses' attention. This is an important message in the story: don't simply stop

---

[16] Richard Forster, "Living Confidently in God" 30 Good Minutes Program #4315, 16 January 2000

to focus on a burning bush itself. Don't let that be the center of your attention. Verse 3 says: "Then Moses said, 'I will now turn aside and see this great sight, why the bush does not burn." Focus on or seek the purpose of the miraculous experience.

He was drawn to the flame, not because he was seeking a spiritual experience—he was at a spiritual low at this point—but because he was curious. It is interesting that God would choose to reveal himself through a flame, since fire, by its very nature is mysterious, at once intriguing and attractive and, in some ways, scary and dangerous. It is equally intriguing that this extraordinary flame is infused into an ordinary bush. It is even more fascinating to think that the ordinary is not overwhelmed and destroyed by the extraordinary. In other words, this is a fire that does not consume; it burns but does not burn up—a curious paradox indeed.

The encounter began, not with Moses invoking the name of God, but with God calling Moses by name! This must have shocked Moses because, by this time, he had so hidden his identity he was sure no one knew him by name. His identity, his dreams, and his sense of self-worth had faded into a distant memory. God called his name from the dancing flame—twice, just to be sure, just like he would call Samuel and then Paul centuries later. I wonder if Moses' heart pounded as he heard his name out in the barren desert.

Like with Moses, God wants to meet you, not when conditions are ideal, but in your natural experience, right where you are. You will note that in this encounter, God does not bring up Moses' past. Instead, He invites him to a loving relationship that will absorb all his past failures. It is as if He is saying, "Moses, I already know you murdered someone, and you have guilt written all over you. Now, get close to the flame and my refining fire will burn away all the negative aspects in your life and reignite your dreams so you can begin to live again."

Lessons from a Successful Failure

This story is a demonstration of the way God deals with us. It hints at a couple details about our journey with God.

Don't stop with the burning bush. Don't let that be the center of your attention.

First, it points to the uncontainable mystery and wonder of the Presence of He who calls us. The life of faith is about being broken open so that a new life can occur. We need to relate to God not as a distant figure giving orders for us to follow, but as a loving father whose life and fire is kindled in us.[17]

Second, it suggests that when we come to God, we begin not as "knowers," but as the known. We are known before we know, named before we name, called before we call, and spoken to before we speak. What seems like our initiative to seek Him turns out to be only a response to a prior initiative taken by the One who created us and knows us perfectly. So in our praying, we are not waking up God and getting His attention. We are being awakened. God is attracting our attention, and we are then responding to the one who is already here. The one all too familiar with our brokenness—only that we didn't realize it![18]

[17] Christians are Christians not because everything is clear or because we have all the answers, but because we sense that Christ's own life—broken, buried, resurrected—and has proved to be uncontainable. It has spread out, kindled, and renewed lives all over the world.

[18] I am sure you remember the story of Hagar in Genesis 16:1-14. Sarah's wife, frustrated by not being able to conceive, gave her maidservant, Hagar, to Abraham to bear then a child. Abraham, a willing victim of his wife, sleeps with Hagar and she conceives. Sarah becomes jealous and sends the hapless girl and her son away to die in the desert. Here the angel of the Lord encounters Hagar and she exclaims: "You are the God who sees me, for she said, I have now seen the one who sees me."

Third, through this encounter with Moses, we see that God wants to be known through a dynamic image (the dancing flame) beyond words, creeds, doctrines, traditions, or denominations. We err when we put God in our neatly defined theologies, in our particular spiritual experiences, or in our denominational groupings—Catholic, Presbyterian, Methodist, Pentecostal-Charismatic-Third Wave, or any other denomination. God wants to be known in the context of a dancing flame—a flame that does not destroy what it touches.

The God of My Grandmother

God wants to be known through a heritage, a tradition, or a story! When Moses responded, God introduced himself in a fascinating way: "I am the God of your father, the God of Abraham, the God of Isaac, and the God of Jacob" (Exodus 3:6). You can know what God is doing or what He will do by looking at what He has done and who He has used in the past.

God wants to be known through a dynamic image-a dancing flame-beyond words, creeds, doctrines, traditions, or church traditions.

In a prayer meeting a number of years ago, I nearly caused a stir and came close to being branded a flaming liberal when I invoked the names of my ancestors—the God of Nyiva (my grandmother), the God of Mbiti (my grandfather) and the God of Ninga (the epical ancestor in my kinship). My ancestors lived through extremely unforgiving conditions: famines, plagues, and many natural calamities. God helped them to adapt, innovate, create, and dream. The circumstances in my life do not take God by surprise. He helped my ancestors, and he will help me as well.

In the encounter with Moses, it is as if God is saying, "You are now encountering the one that your ancestors have encountered over many generations. This may be a new experience to you, but it is not unprecedented. I have done this many times down the centuries; it is now your time to enter into a conversation your ancestors participated in."

Night of Struggle

Moses' experience echoed another encounter of his distant ancestor Jacob (Genesis 28:10-22; 32:22-32):

> Jacob left Beersheba and set out for Harran. When he

reached a certain place, he stopped for the night because the sun had set. Taking one of the stones there, he put it under his head and lay down to sleep. He had a dream in which he saw a stairway resting on the earth, with its top reaching to heaven, and the angels of God were ascending and descending on it. There above it stood the LORD, and he said: "I am the LORD, the God of your father Abraham and the God of Isaac. I will give you and your descendants the land on which you are lying. Your descendants will be like the dust of the earth, and you will spread out to the west and to the east, to the north and to the south. All peoples on earth will be blessed through you and your offspring. I am with you and will watch over you wherever you go, and I will bring you back to this land. I will not leave you until I have done what I have promised you." When Jacob awoke from his sleep, he thought, "Surely the LORD is in this place, and I was not aware of it." He was afraid and said, "How awesome is this place! This is none other than the house of God; this is the gate of heaven."

Jacob's encounter with God was in a dream of a ladder reaching to the sky instead of a burning bush in the desert. Notice the origination of the angelic activity. They were ascending and descending. Is it possible that there is much angelic activity all around us, and we don't even perceive it? It is very easy for us to get caught up in the "busyness" of life and fail to notice what is going on around us. At other times, we miss our moments because we have our emotions deeply buried in the past. Could-haves, would-haves, should-haves preoccupy our minds to the point of missing present opportunities. "If we are paying attention to our lives," T.D. Jakes wrote, "we will live with fewer regrets and transform the ticking of the clocks hands into priceless treasure."[19]

Someone once said that life is what happens when we are busy making other plans!

I am afraid that, many times, we are like Elisha's servant:

Elisha's servant got up early, and when he went out, he saw an army with horses and chariots all around the city. The servant said to Elisha,

[19] T.D Jakes, He-Motions: Even Strong Men Struggle (Penguin Group (USA) Inc. New York, 2004), p, 85

"Oh, my master, what can we do?" Elisha said, "Don't be afraid. The army that fights for us is larger than the one against us." Then Elisha prayed, "LORD, open my servant's eyes, and let him see." The LORD opened the eyes of the young man, and he saw that the mountain was full of horses and chariots of fire all around Elisha (2 Kings 6:17)

Looking at the Christian faith from the outside, many describe it as dull, legalistic, unintelligent, and unappealing; but from the inside, it is something else altogether. Through the eyes of the faithful, the Christian life is beautiful, majestic, powerful, and full of joy and meaning.

Seen through the eyes of fear and skepticism, the situation at Dothan looked hopeless. No wonder the unbelieving servant sighed, "Alas, my master! What shall we do?" Elisha, facing the identical situation, saw things differently. He said, "Do not fear, for those who are with us are more than those who are with them." He was viewing the situation with the eyes of faith. Through the eyes of God, the horses and chariots of divine protection were clearly visible. Elisha asked God to give his servant the same 20/20 vision on the spiritual eye chart, so he too would not be afraid.

Awaking from his sleep, Jacob cried out, "God was in this place and I did not even know it!" It is possible for us to sleep through our opportunities and—to lament like Jacob, saying, "God was here and I missed the party!"

Do you recall that little sadness that greets you in the morning? Maybe it's because you are not doing what you are supposed to be doing. You are not living the life you are supposed to be living. Could it be it's because, like so many in our day, you spent time regretting missed opportunities?

Power with God and with Men

Many years later, Jacob had another encounter with God, alone and at night. Our fear of being alone drives us to noise and to crowds. We keep up constant stream of words, even if they are insane. We have not learned the art of being alone without being lonely.

> ***Before God can get through to you, you must quiet your heart enough to discern that small voice telling us, this is the way, walk in it***

This time, God manifested himself not through a burning bush or a ladder reaching to heaven, but as a powerful night assailant determined to bring Jacob to the point of surrender in a wrestling match. The Bible records:

> *That night Jacob got up and took his two wives, his two female servants and his eleven sons and crossed the ford of the Jabbok. After he had sent them across the stream, he sent over all his possessions. So Jacob was left alone, and a man wrestled with him till daybreak. When the man saw that he could not overpower him, he touched the socket of Jacob's hip so that his hip was wrenched as he wrestled with the man. Then the man said, "Let me go, for it is daybreak." But Jacob replied, "I will not let you go unless you bless me." The man asked him, "What is your name?" "Jacob," he answered. Then the man said, "Your name will no longer be Jacob, but Israel, because you have struggled with God and with humans and have overcome." Jacob said, "Please tell me your name." But he replied, "Why do you ask my name?" Then he blessed him there. So Jacob called the place Peniel, saying, "It is because I saw God face to face, and yet my life*

was spared." The sun rose above him as he passed Peniel, and he was limping because of his hip. Therefore to this day the Israelites do not eat the tendon attached to the socket of the hip, because the socket of Jacob's hip was touched near the tendon.

(Genesis 32:22-29)

Alone with God

At the time of this encounter, Jacob was a fugitive on the run. He had been in the school of hard knocks for twenty years. Though he believed in God, he was out of fellowship with Him. However, he was about to discover that God did not love him for what he was, but for what He could make out of him.

Now, God finally had Jacob exactly where He wanted him: alone. It took a while because Jacob didn't want to be alone. You can tell when people are running from God because they don't want to be alone. They hide in the crowd or in too much activity—even religious activity.

One of the greatest threats we face as members of a community is the *"massification"* of the individual (if I can coin that word). For people who do not want to face themselves, the crowd becomes a sink of cowardice in which individuals are relieved of personal responsibility and will think and commit acts and hold to beliefs they would not dare do on their own. They think (if they think at all) and act as members of a political party, a denomination, a race, a class, or a tribe. They don't want to face themselves, and they can't face God.

> *Settle yourself in solitude and you will come upon him in yourself*
>
> *Teresa of Avila*

Before God can get through to you, you must quiet your heart enough to discern that small, still voice, saying:

"If you go the wrong way—to the right or to the left—you will hear a voice behind you saying, 'this is the right way. You should go this way.'" Isaiah 30:21 (NCV). Like a GPS always alerts us to turns on our journey, the Spirit of God is constant in His guidance for the directions we take and the way we walk in life.

Back to Jacob's experience, verse 24 tells us that Jacob was finally alone, and he had a confrontation with God. Here, he came face-to-face with the angel of the Lord, and they engaged in a wrestling match. It is interesting to note that the wrestling went on all night and in silence, not a word was uttered.

Silence

When I read this story, I see a deeper sense of what is happening. Beyond the sheer strength of his night assailant, Jacob is engulfed in silence! Now, it took me a while to get this. Our generation does little to help us to appreciate the language of silence. Our enemy, the Devil, majors in three things: hurry, worry, and noise. Thomas Merton correctly observed, "We put words between ourselves and things." He continued:

> *Even God has become another conceptual unreality in a no-man's- land of language that no longer serves as means of communication with reality. The solitary life, being silent, clears away the smokescreen of words that we have laid down between our minds and things. In solitude we remain face to face with the naked being of things. And yet we find*

> *that the nakedness of reality which we have feared is neither a matter of terror or of shame. It is clothed in the friendly communion of silence, and this silence is related to love.*[20]

I have a few friends whose calls I avoid or whose presence I do not enjoy. Why? Words! They are too wordy. They control the conversation with words. I have been on the phone with such friends, and the call that should have taken a few minutes goes on forever. They will not pause to allow me time to share my thoughts. You, too, know people like this, but as Richard Rohr noted:

> *Silence is the language of God, and the only language deep enough to absorb all the contradictions and failures that we are holding against ourselves. God loves us silently because God has no case to make against us. The silent communion absorbs our self-hatred, as every lover knows.*[21]

Beyond the physical wrestling, God's silence is soaking up Jacob's

[20] Quoted in Jane Redmont, When in Doubt Sin (Notre Dame, IN: Sorin, 2008), p. 76

[21] Richard Rohr, Simplicity: The Freedom of Letting Go (New York: Crossroad, 2004) p. 97

self-loathing, doubts, despair, and failures. To be sure, it wasn't Jacob wrestling with the Lord. It was the Lord wrestling with Jacob. The Lord started it, and it could have been over very quickly, but the Lord wanted Jacob to prevail. It is the same thing that happens when a father is arm wrestling with his son. The father allows the lad to win a few times and lets the play to go on for a while longer. In the same way, God did not want to overcome Jacob. He was trying to do something with this man that He loves so much. In the same way, God does not want to overpower us. He wants to work with us to create the future he dreams for us. In this sense, our future is partially settled. God wants us to join him in creating the future we desire. He invites us to wrestle with the issues until life yields its ultimate meaning. The greater the struggle, the more glorious the triumph!

Crippled by God

Finally, when they had wrestled all night, without saying a word, the angel touched the hollow of Jacob's thigh and crippled him. Now, when a wrestler's legs are gone, he cannot do much. This is the strongest muscle for a wrestler. Without it, he cannot pivot his foot or maneuver his body. Jacob was crippled; his final weapon was finally taken away. If all his plans and strength had failed, at least he could have run. Now, he couldn't even do that. God brought him to the place of utter, absolute, and complete brokenness and dependence. He had only one option: hold on to this night assailant![22]

Blessed by God

The Angel said to this crippled man, "Let me go." Ironically, the word "Jacob" means "that which grabs; that which holds." Jacob was still grasping, but this time, for the first time in his life, he grabbed the right thing, or shall I say, the right one. He got ahold of the Lord.

> ***To be sure, it wasn't Jacob wrestling with the Lord. It was the Lord wrestling with Jacob. The Lord started it, and it could have been over very quickly, but the Lord wanted Jacob to win the wrestling match!***

He said, *"Oh God, I need you. God, I will not let you go unless you bless me."* God had been waiting to hear those words for so long and, at that moment, something wonderful took place.

[22] When God takes away something from your hand, don't for once think he is depriving you. He is simply emptying your hand so he can give you something better.

Like Moses in the burning bush, Jacob's impulse was to get the name of this mysterious Being. Interestingly, the wrestler, concealed in darkness, did not recapitulate, but turned the tables on Jacob and demanded that Jacob declare his name instead. For all intents and purposes, God knew Jacob's name, but He wanted Jacob to confess his name that further meant *"liar, cheater, crook, fraud, schemer, conman, and deceiver."* After the admission of who he truly was, God gave him a new name, Israel, which means "a prince of God." He became a prince of God because he finally came to the end of himself. You see, God wanted to bless Jacob, not hurt him. God crippled him so that he might crown him. God broke him so that he might bless him.

Do you know why many of us are not yet truly blessed? Why we have so many false starts? We have not yet been truly broken. Men throw broken things away, but God never uses anything until he first breaks it. You'll never show me anybody who has been or will be mightily used of God who has not first been broken. There is no blessedness without brokenness. There is no crown without a cross. There is no throne without the thorns!

Walking with a Limp

For the rest of his life, Jacob had to use a crutch or staff to walk. The encounter he had was not just a spiritual high, similar to hyped up emotions at a revival. His condition wasn't just something that could be fixed or reversed. This was permanent.

The Bible says in Hebrews 11:21: "By faith Jacob, when he was a dying, blessed both the sons of Joseph and worshipped leaning upon the top of his staff." Here he was, 147 years old and still leaning. Jacob had finally learned to lean. Like the Apostle Paul, he discovered that God's strength is most clearly seen through our weakness:

But he said to me, "My grace is enough for you. When you are weak, my power is made perfect in you." So I am very happy to brag about my weaknesses. Then Christ's power can live in me. For this reason, I am happy when I have weaknesses, insults, hard times, sufferings, and all kinds of troubles for Christ. Because when I am weak, then I am truly strong. (2 Corinthians 12:9-10 New Century Version).

Jacob's defiance had turned to reliance. He who had, until a few moments ago, been trying to make life work without the Lord, finally realized how impossible it was for him to function without God. The striking picture of the sun rising on the once self-sufficient Jacob as he limped on his way—now the proud bearer of a new name (Israel)—should never be forgotten. When God blesses you, it is always the dawn of a new day. God had dealt graciously with His servant, and there would never be a day as long as he lived that Israel would forget that his strength had come from his surrender. As he sank low on one hip and rose strongly on the other, each step was a testament to the night he learned that "the way up is down, and the way down is up!"

> *When God takes away something from your hand, don't for once think he is depriving you. He is simply emptying your hand so he can give you something better.*

The Great Paradox

The deepest longings of the human heart can and must be changed if we are to become all that God designed us to be. Our deviant longings are cruel masters; even where the object of desire is a good thing, the status of the desire usurps God and tries to dethrone His eternal purposes. Our cravings should be exposed in order that we may more richly know God as the Savior, Lover, and Converter of the human soul. God would have us long for Him more than we long for material things. To make us truly human, God must change what we want; we must learn to want the things Jesus wanted.

"Those who die to self, find self. Those who die to their cravings will receive many times as much in this age, and, in the age to come, eternal life." (Luke 18:29) They will find new passions worth living for. If we crave happiness, we will receive misery. If we crave to be loved, we will receive rejection. If we crave power, we will receive scorn. If we crave control, we will receive chaos. If we crave reputation, we will receive humiliation. However, if we long for God and His wisdom and mercy, we will receive God and His wisdom and mercy. Along the way, sooner or later, we will also receive happiness, love, meaning, order, and glory.

God's Word will keep you from sin or sin will keep you from God's Word. He is no fool who gives up what he cannot keep to gain what he cannot lose

Jim Eliot

We live by dying. We are victorious when we surrender. We gain by losing.[23] Jim Elliot (1927-1956), missionary to the Auca Indians of Ecuador, is credited with expressing this classic piece of wisdom: "He is no fool who gives what he cannot keep to gain what he cannot lose." The entire quote reads, "God's Word will keep you from sin or sin will keep you from God's Word. He is no fool who gives up what he cannot keep to gain what he cannot lose."[24]

---

[23] Jesus said, "For whoever wants to save his life will lose it, but whoever loses his life for me and for the gospel will save it" -Mark 8.35 (TNIV).

[24] The best source for quotes by Jim Eliot is his biography written by his wife Elisabeth Elliot-In The Shadow of the Almighty, published by Harper and Row in 1958. It contains extensive quotes from his personal journals

CHAPTER 6

Not Without a Doubt

Doubt, like a starless night of the soul, a low point in our lives when faith seems to have ebbed and retreated forever, is a reality we all must face. Growing up in Kenya as a young Christian, I was taught that doubt was a bad thing. In fact there was a popular song to enforce this belief:

Why worry, when you can pray
Trust Jesus, he knows the way
Don't be a doubting Thomas
Just lean upon his promise
Why worry, worry, worry,
When you can pray!

> ***Modest doubt is called the beacon of the wise***
>
> ***William Shakespeare***

Contrary to popular belief, at the heart of a life filled with unanswered questions lies the very nature of the Christian faith. Our faith is not about an adherence to a set of creeds and intellectual ideas we have memorized; it's about a dynamic relationship with Christ.

Hanging On When You Can't See His Plan

The truth is that nearly all of us experience those dry, dark, and difficult times in our lives when it seems like God is nowhere within a thousand miles from where we are. In those moments, God doesn't seem real, and it is difficult to keep going, let alone keep growing. In the ebb and flow of our life, these low points are often linked to traumatic events: death of a loved one, a broken relationship, financial upheaval, prolonged illness, and questions raised by pain and suffering in the world. The problem is made worse when we insist on having all our questions answered immediately.

However, then there are times when these doubts seem to pop up from nowhere. It may be sunny and bright outside, but inside you feel dark, cloudy, gray and empty. As a pastor and spiritual guide, I deal with doubt on a daily basis. And not just doubt in other people, but my own doubts as well! I too struggle with my own faith, even in the midst of an active ministry. However, in the words of Andre Crouch's song, "Through it all, I have learned to trust in Jesus. I have learned to trust in God..." This means we trust Him even when we can't trace His footsteps. I have come to see doubt as the gateway to spiritual growth. Resisting temptation is a constant battle we face as Christians, but avoiding or eliminating doubt can dull our faith.

As a professor of religion and philosophy at different Christian universities, I am deeply disturbed by how shallow and superficial our Christian answers are in the face of profound and honest questions that bedevil our planet. In many cases, we sidestep the questions, or we reshape them to give answers to questions that no one is asking! To add to this confusion, we have voices from the Pentecostal/Charismatic/Third Wave theologies, whose only solution to difficult questions of life can be compared to playing American football; they punt everything to faith!

I have since wanted to help Christians find a deeper, more thoughtful, honest faith. My desire is to assist spiritual seekers in achieving answers to their probing questions that will aid them to come to a faith that is honest, vibrant, and deepening. Doubts develop around three simple questions: how, why, and where? How can two seemingly contradicting realities exist side by side? Why does a good God allow bad things to happen? Where was God when all this was happening to me? We struggle with what theologians call God's immanence (nearness or accessibility) and God's transcendence (complete otherness).

Magical Religion[25]

When people experience a breakdown in the spiritual life, it is often because they fail to hold this dynamism in tandem. We must forever live with the tension of God's immanence and His transcendence. If we resolve the tension only on the side of transcendence or otherness, God becomes distant—at first, a kind of remote deity (as in African and other folk religions), then an abstract principle, then an impersonal cosmic energy (New Age spiritualities), and eventually God may disappear altogether, leaving us in a world lacking meaning, purpose, or direction (deism). In such world, Moses' bush no longer burns, Jacob's

[25] While we should remain open to accepting fresh expressions of spiritual experiences, we need to be watch out for the kind of faith that puts too much emphasis on subjective feelings.

ladder leans against the wrong wall, and his mysterious night assailant becomes just another thug or mugger. We call, but nobody is at home. We pray, but no one is on the other side to listen to our prayers.

In magical religion, God becomes too much the chum or watchdog, a mascot and a genie that comes obediently when a few religious incantations are repeated

On the other hand, if we resolve the tension on the side of immanence or nearness, God becomes too much the chum or watchdog, a mascot and a genie that comes obediently when a few religious incantations are repeated![26] When this happens, prayer becomes much like abracadabra—those magical incantations of the magicians on stage that are believed to have healing powers. Religion begins looking much like superstition and witchcraft, and preachers begin sounding like sanctified magicians.

---

[26] McLaren, Naked Spirituality, P. 43

Magical religion in this mode often turns homicidal and genocidal because God conveniently hates the same people His followers hate and is happy to see them suffer. Rather than loving our enemies, we are glad to "nuke 'em." Such magical religion subjects people to a sort of spiritual terrorism. People get a constant diet of fire and brimstone sermons such that God as the Terminator theology is thundered Sunday after Sunday! Surprisingly, people flock to these types of churches to have guilt heaped on them by preachers who seem to speak with pontifical authority.

Doubting Saints

Doubt is no stranger to people of faith. One of the most well known passages in the Bible is Matthew 28:18-20. This passage is referred to by some as the Great Commission—Christ's marching orders to the Church:

> *"Then Jesus came to them and said, 'All authority in heaven and on earth is given to me. So go and make followers of all people in the world. Baptize them in the name of the Father and the Son and the Holy Spirit.*

Teach them to obey everything that I have taught you, and I will be with you always, even until the end of this age.'"

(Every Day Bible: New Century Version)

I have preached from this passage many times in mission conferences. It is one of the main reasons I resigned my job from Royal Insurance Company of East Africa to become an itinerant evangelist and later professor of religion and philosophy. Arguably, it has become the international rallying cry for Christians everywhere.

There is a slight problem, though. We have distorted the original thrust of the message. All students of literature and any serious and intellectually honest students of the Bible know that "a text without a context is a pretext for proof text." Anyone can lift a text out of context and make it say what he wants it to say to support his point. Unfortunately, this is what preachers have done with Matthew 28:18-20. When we consider just two verses preceding the Great Commission, a new light is shed on the meaning and thrust of Matthew 28:16-20. They read:

> Then the eleven disciples went away into Galilee, to the mountain, which Jesus had appointed for them. When they saw Him, they worshiped Him; but some doubted. And Jesus came and spoke to them, saying, "All authority has been given to Me in heaven and on earth. Go therefore and make disciples of all the nations, baptizing them in the name of the Father and of the Son and of the Holy Spirit, teaching them to observe all things that I have commanded you; and lo, I am with you always, even to the end of the age." Amen.

Do you see the difference those two preceding verses make? Notice how those three words *"but some doubted"* changes the focus. The context tells us that eleven disciples went to Galilee to the place Christ had directed them to go. "Some doubted" refers to a few of the original disciples. We are not told who or how many. This is good because if we knew their identity, we would begin to theorize why they doubted and to somehow teach people NOT to be like "those" doubters. It is ironic that, after all those years of living with Christ, watching him heal the sick, hearing his profound teachings (including his prediction that He would suffer), seeing Him die on the cross and resurrect after three days, they still doubted.

Jesus stood there and knew their thinking and understood their doubting. Here were the people with whom He was going to entrust His worldwide message of redemption, and they doubted Him. He was about to put it all in their hands—the incarnation, the teachings, the suffering, the miracles, the death on the cross, the final plan for redeeming God's creation. All was going to be placed on their shoulders.

> ***The greater the artist, the greater the doubt . . .***
> ***Perfect confidence is granted to the less talented***
> ***as a consolation prize.***
>
> ***Robert Hughes***

If Christ were somewhat like us, He would have responded angrily, "Guys, I am livid. This doubt you are displaying is a showstopper. I am not entrusting anything to you until you settle those questions and reassure me that you are 100% convinced of who I am and my plan of redemption." Instead, He sent them out with their doubts.

> *Lord, in the daytime stars can be seen from the deepest wells, and the deeper the well the brighter the stars shine; Let me find your light in my darkness, your life in my death, your joy in my sorrow, your grace in my sin your riches in my poverty, your glory in my valley*
>
> *Author Unknown*

This passage is programmatic and announces a very important way in which God works us in our weaknesses. Accurately interpreted, the Great Commission passage brings us face to face with this reality: ***doubt is part of our Christian faith, and Jesus even uses people who go through periods of doubt.*** It acknowledges that doubt has a way of bubbling up to the surface when we are faced with hardships. You should not see your doubt as a lack of commitment or a sign of weakness. Scripture gives evidence that even the most devoted must face doubts in their walk with God.

This is what happened to John the Baptist when he was in prison. Scripture records:

> *John's followers told him about all these things. He called for two of his followers and sent them to the Lord to ask, "Are you the One who is to come, or should we wait for someone else?" When the men came to Jesus, they said, "John the Baptist sent us to you with this question: 'Are you the One who is to come, or should we wait for someone else?'"*
>
> (Luke 7:18-20)

This is one of the most amazing Scriptures in the Word of God. John the Baptist had prepared the people for the coming of the Messiah. Jesus said, concerning John the Baptist, in Matthew 11:11, "Among them that are born of women, there has not risen a greater than John the Baptist..." It was John who baptized Jesus (Matthew 3:14). It was John who proclaimed to the people in John 1:29, "Behold the lamb of God, who takes away the sin of the world."

Yet, we see this giant of the faith doubting whether Christ was the messiah or whether they should look for another. Had he forgotten the day he baptized Jesus? Had he forgotten the sight of the Holy Spirit descending on Jesus like a dove? Had he forgotten the voice he heard from heaven declaring that Christ was God's beloved son in whom He was well pleased? What about his own message to the people that after him will come one who will baptize with the Holy Spirit and with fire?

Disappointed by God

A similar account is recorded regarding the disciples on the road to Emmaus. This story is preserved for us in Luke's Gospel and is one of my favorite New Testament accounts. It shows a side of being a follower of Christ that not too many of us want to admit exists. We do not want to admit that, sometimes, we are disappointed by God. Not too many of us will admit to that, at least, not in those exact words. We dare not. It would sound…well… blasphemous.

Disappointment is there alright, deep down inside, and what I want to ask of you now, before I go any further, is this: if you are disappointed with God, acknowledge it, to both yourself and to Him, and then join me on the path that was blazed for you and all the others like you over 2,000 years ago. This path goes by the name of the "Road to Emmaus!"

> ***Why hurry home? What would be there: a dark house, a dead candle on the table, and tasteless bread, stale water?***

In Luke 24: 13-32, we learn about how Christ, after His resurrection, appeared on the road to a place called Emmaus with His disciples and Cleopas. Why were these disciples leaving Jerusalem? Why hurry home? What would be there except for a dark house, a dead candle on the table, tasteless bread, or stale water? By their own admission, so much was happening in Jerusalem. Jesus had died alright, but there were rumors of angels who said He had been seen alive. The body was missing from the grave (v. 23-24). Fresh news was coming in by the hour. So why leave Jerusalem? Was it because of fear?

The first thing that strikes me about these dejected disciples is their sheer wistfulness. When a stranger, the resurrected Christ, joined them and asked what they were talking about, they "were looking sad." And when pressed about their sadness, they told the stranger about Jesus. "We had hoped…" they began (:21), "that it was He who was going to redeem Israel." What a weight of disappointment in those first three words. Are these words that perhaps characterize your Christian walk? "I had hoped…"

Doubts are like ants in the pants of faith.

They keep it awake and moving!

Are you a wistful Christian? Am I? Are we standing still, looking sad? Are we stuck? Are we stuck in what John Bunyan referred to as the "Slough of Despond?"[27]

Years ago, we started a journey, and way back then, we were full of excitement, anticipation, and hope. We were alive to God, committed to Him, full of faith and fervor. However, then—

[27] In John Bunyan's Pilgrims Progress, one of the interesting aspects of Pilgrims journey to the cross is the Slough of Despondent, a place into which Christian and Pliable both stumble.

wham! Something went wrong. Somehow, over the years, our fervor died, our faith became mainly a matter of talk, and our hope grew dim. Our dreams were crushed.

Why? How? Well, maybe your prayers didn't seem to rise above your nose or the answers were not what you expected. Maybe things happened that you didn't think should have happened to you; after all, you prayed, you supported God's work and tried to treat others right. Maybe we felt let down by God or even ignored by Him, so a disappointment with God set in, like with Cleopas and his companions on a road from Jerusalem.

Perhaps we, like Cleopas and his companions, are trudging along, heads down, shoulders stooped, united in our disappointment. However, in their story, something refreshing happens. Jesus Himself draws near and walks with them. Our disappointment with God doesn't drive Him further away; we might expect it to, but it doesn't. On the contrary, it seems to be the very thing that draws God closer to us in the person of Jesus. In fact, if you are disappointed with God, I can safely promise you that Jesus has drawn near and is walking alongside you, even in your doubt.

Healthy doubt can serve as radar that detects error. Without it, we would be gullible, naïve, and just plain stupid—not exactly the spiritual qualities we would wish to have. Doubt, I must warn is not always good. There is a dark despairing doubt—an exaggerated and self-destructive doubt that leads to defeat, depression, and self-sabotage. Active imagination is good in itself, but when it gets out of control, it turns into a sort of schizophrenia. It is good to be sensitive, and anger is a necessary emotion, but too much of either can lead to depression.

Doubt works in the same way. Once it spirals out of control, it becomes disbelief, a hardened heart, and an arrogant cynicism. Like guilt, doubt, the late Christian philosopher Francis Schaeffer said, "is like a watchdog: useful to have around to warn of lurking danger. However, if the watchdog turns and attacks the homeowner, it needs to be restrained."[28]

Ants in the Pants

So, is doubt good or bad? The answer is it's both! Doubts, wrote

---

[28] Francis Schaeffer, quoted in Adventures in Missing the Point by Brian D. McLaren and Tony Campolo (Zondervan: Grand Rapids, MI 2003), p. 244.

Frederick Buechner in his book *Wishful Thinking, are "the ants in the pants of faith. They keep it awake and moving."*[29] Being awake and moving is simply spiritual growth to which we, as Christians, claim to be committed. Spiritual growth implies that five years from now, your set of beliefs will hopefully be different from today's. Your beliefs will be more fine-tuned, more tested, more balanced, and more examined. Unless, of course, you are a red-blooded conservative evangelical like many of my seminary friends with whom I spur on occasion with a range of social and theological issues. Many are afraid that openness to doubt will lead to liberalism. What is more dangerous? Holding on to false beliefs or holding out the possibility that there is something better?

Imagine for a moment that you were a white Christian living in the southern states in the United States during the 1860s. Your church taught you that blacks were under the curse of Ham and, therefore, inferior to whites and deserving of being slaves to their white superiors. The Bible is quoted extensively to buttress this belief as a moral absolute, and to doubt it, is treason not only

[29] Buechner, Frederick, Wishful Thinking (Harper Collins: NY 1973) p. 38.

against the state, but against the church as well. Would you not agree that a person would be a better Christian for doubting that teaching?

Your doubt can be a doorway to spiritual growth. Unfortunately, like many avenues of growth, it is painful. At the heart of a life

Your doubt can be a doorway to spiritual growth.
Unfortunately, like many avenues of growth, it is painful.
At the heart of a life filled with unanswered questions
lies the very essence of Christianity.

filled with unanswered questions lies the very essence of Christianity. Our faith is about being in a living, dynamic relationship with Christ, not in giving mental ascent to a set of doctrines and creeds. At Fountain of Life, where I am the lead pastor, I often remind our congregation that *here, we have no creed but Christ; doctrine divides, love unites.* In our church, we admit openly that we do not have all the answers. However, that does not keep us from becoming obedient followers of Christ.

Chapter 7

Encouragement: Handling Failure

I once read a story of an elderly lady who did her shopping in a busy mall. When she returned to her car, she found four young men sitting in it! She dropped her shopping bags and pulled out her concealed weapon and started to scream at them at the top of her voice. She assured them that she knew how to use her gun and that she surely would if she needed to. The four men didn't wait around to see if she could shoot or if the gun was loaded. They got out of the car and ran like mad. Satisfied, the lady loaded her shopping bags into the trunk and climbed into the driver's seat. She had a small problem; however, her key wouldn't fit in the ignition!

> ***People say you can't unscramble eggs.***
>
> ***True, but you can make omelet!***

Taking a closer look, she discovered her car, which was identical to the one in which she was sitting, was parked four spaces farther down. Terribly embarrassed, she loaded her bags into her car and, unable to find any of the four young men at which she had pointed her gun, she drove to the police station. She told the sergeant the story and he laughed heartily before pointing to the other end of the counter where four males, white as ghosts, were reporting a car-jacking by a crazed elderly woman with a loaded gun. No charges were filled.

Like this mistaken woman, we also make mistakes. Sometimes we fail because of ignorance, but other times, we fail out of mere rebellion. Take heart. God is on your side. He does not want charges against you. He wants you to overcome your sinful nature and enjoy the abundant life He created for you to live. Do you remember how you felt when you started your life with God? The old had gone, and the new had come? Not so fast. Satan has had his eyes on you like never before. He will quickly try to use your old nature (the flesh)[30] to get back in your life with a slip here or a wrong turn there. Suddenly, you realize that you

[30] The Bible teaches that our human nature is inherently rebellious against God. We inherited this nature from Adam and, unfortunately, it was not eradicated when we became Christians. It is still within us, but we are no longer forced to obey its dictates. Our human nature motivates the selfishness we sometimes feel, the complaining about our circumstances, the petty jealousies, the elbowing for power in the church, the office and in our families, the lure of pornography, and all the rest. Spirit, however, does enable us to live free of the flesh.

are struggling with habits and thoughts you assumed that being a believer would remove from your life.

The truth is, you belong to your choice! You have two natures within you. From the time you were born, you had the first nature. When you are born again, you have a new nature. Think of your first, or old, nature as gravity, always in effect to pull you downward. Think of the new nature as the wings of an airplane to keep you soaring, functioning, growing, and causing the love of God to flow through you.

> *"For the desires of the flesh (old nature) are against the Spirit (new nature), and the desires of the Spirit are against the flesh; for these are opposed to each other; to prevent you from doing what you would."*
>
> (Galatians 5:17)

As long as you live, these two natures will be locked in conflict. Your choices decide which nature will control your life. When we fail, God does not want us to quit and give up trying to live like Christ. That's our natural tendency, but God has a better idea. Look at this verse:

"The LORD upholds all those who fall and gives a fresh start to those ready to quit."

Psalm 145:14 (NIV)

It was a great day, the day I came to the realization that I was forgiven. Not just for the sins of the past, but for all sins: past, and present, and future. More than anything else, a lack of this understanding keeps people imprisoned by past failures. King David, of whom God testified that he was a man after his own heart, struggled just like we do with failure, until he prayed:

God, be merciful to me
because you are loving.
Because you are always ready to be merciful,
wipe out all my wrongs.
Wash away all my guilt
and make me clean again.
I know about my wrongs,
and I can't forget my sin.

Psalm 51:1-3[31]

[31] Tradition ascribes this Psalm to David in the context of his sin with Bathsheba (2 Sam. 11-12). Here, David was actually guilty of a whole chain of sins. Lust led to adultery, adultery to deception, and deception to murder. In his attempt to cover his tracks, he only dug the pit deeper. In this sense, David was no different from all of us.

Other translations render verse 3 with the words, ***"my sin is ever before me."*** In other words, David was plagued by ceaseless sin consciousness! How dreadful it is to be plagued perennially by a haunting presence? How awful it is to be under surveillance morning, noon, and night by an ever-threatening eye?

How awful it is to have your forgetfulness declare no vacancy, while your memory makes room for unlimited lodging of unwanted guests. How awful it is to be stalked from the doing of deeds to our death by agonizing actualities, not empty apparitions that bespeak our wretchedness.

Counting Sheep or Counting Sins?

King David seems to admit, upon first read, that, while reclining on his bed, this plaguing presence would press itself upon his subconscious, and it would turn dreams into nightmares, restfulness into restlessness; and, instead of counting sheep, he would spend even his resting hours counting sins.

David does not window dress his condition. He acknowledges that his active imagination is drowning him in the pit of his past sin. Bible scholars agree that this was after he had committed adultery with Uriah's wife, Bathsheba. As though that was not awful enough, he plotted and had Uriah killed. Consequently, the first child conceived out of his union with Bathsheba died. Thankfully, our failures should not have the last word. God has the last word and the word after that. It may have taken a while, but David waited on the Lord, and help did finally come. We read:

I waited patiently for the LORD.
He turned to me and heard my cry.
He lifted me out of the pit of destruction,
out of the sticky mud.
He stood me on a rock
and made my feet steady.
He put a new song in my mouth,
a song of praise to our God.
Many people will see this and worship him.
Then they will trust the LORD.
Psalm 40:1-3

God heard David's cry and rescued him from the *"pit of noise"* or *"the pit of tumult."* In ancient Israel, people used to trap wild animals by digging a pit in their path. Jackals, lions, and other wild beasts would fall into this pit. Thieves and robbers unfamiliar with the terrain would occasionally fall into this pit. One can only imagine the noise coming from this pit of destruction! You and I can climb out of our pit of noise and plant our feet on solid foundation as we follow God's blue print for handling failure. Here are some practical steps to take when you fail and you feel like quitting.

1. Admit you have failed. Let's do a reality check here. I fail often. I am living proof that well meaning Christians do fail. Not once, but repeatedly, and many times with intent. I don't fall into sin. Many times, I walk into it with my eyes wide open. We all fail, but the secret of the spiritual life, I have come to learn, is in desiring to actually be more spiritual than I appear to be. Conversely, the secret to hypocrisy is in desiring to appear more spiritual than you actually are. Thus, Richard Rohr was correct when he said, "If there is such as thing as human perfection, it seems to emerge precisely from how we handle the imperfection that is everywhere, especially our own. So forget 'Holier than thou. I'm seeking to appear holier than moi.'"[32] Jokingly, but with a great deal of seriousness, Father Damascus said, "Don't worry about purifying your motives. Simply know that that aren't pure, and proceed."[33] When I try not to appear holier, better, and stronger than I actually am, I keep the life-giving connection with God intact and unbroken.

2. Assess why you failed. All sin begins in our "thought life." Failure never just happens. This is how Jesus, the greatest teacher who ever lived, explained it:

> *"It is the thought life that defiles you. For from within, out of a person's heart, come evil thoughts, sexual immorality, theft, murder, adultery, greed, wickedness, deceit, eagerness for lustful pleasure, envy, slander, pride, and foolishness. All these vile things come from within; they are what defile you."*
>
> Mark 7:20-23 (NLT)

[32] Rhor Richard, p. 8

[33] Quoted in Jane Redmont, When in Doubt, Sing (Notre Dame, IN: Sorin, 2008), p. 100

3. Ask God for forgiveness. "If we confess our sin to him, he is faithful and just to forgive us and to cleanse us from all wrong." (1 John 1:9) Did you get that? Thoroughly clean, completely forgiven. Isn't that good news? Think of it this way. Is it possible to be partially clean? If you went to a restaurant, would you accept eating from a slightly clean plate with partially clean silverware? Can a woman be just a little bit pregnant? Clean or dirty, pregnant or not, there can be no middle ground. *God says that when we confess our failures, he forgives us and we are clean, so none of the dirt is left.* God makes life complete when you place all the pieces before Him, not when you get your act together.

God makes life complete when you place all the pieces before him, not when you get your act together

We talk much about asking for forgiveness, but many of us never realy act on our conviction. Unconfessed sin keeps us believing we are okay as is. Confessing and receiving God's forgivenness is as vital to our growth, as breathing is to our existence. The Devil knows this and will do anything to stop us from acting on our feelings. C.S. Lewis put it well in his Screwtape Letters. The senior devil, Screwtape, gives the following advice to the junior tempter, Wormwood, in the matter of how Wormwood should attempt to undermine the faith and repentance of a young Christian:

"It remains to consider how we can retrieve this disaster. The great thing is to prevent his doing anything. As long as he does not convert it into action, it does not matter how much he thinks about this new repentance ***(emphasis mine)***. Let the little brute wallow in it. Let him, if he has any bent that way, write a book about it; that is often an excellent way of sterilizing the seeds which the Enemy plants in a human soul. Let him do anything but act. No amount of piety in his imagination and affections will harm us if we can keep it out of his will. As one of the humans has said, active habits are strengthened by repetition but passive ones are weakened. The more often he feels without acting, the less he will be able ever to act, and, in the long run, the less he will be able to feel (emphasis mine)."

The full development of repentance (***Metanoia*** or *change of* *mind*) in the process of cleansing involves breaking up every aspect of conformity that is not in alignment with God's will and the increasing the transformation of our lives by the Holy Spirit's renewing work in our minds. (Romans 12:2)

God wants to make the rest of your life

the best of your life!

4. Access your future. God is saying, it is not so much where you have been that counts, as it is the direction of your heart, or where you are headed. That's what really counts. *Do not cling to past events or dwell on what happened long ago, for God said, "Watch for the* ***new thing*** *I'm going to do."* Isaiah 43:18-19 (TEV)

God's love is full of surprises. Just when our failures take us to the brink of hopelessness, God has another "new thing" for us to hear. With all of the love of His being, He declares, *"I, even I, am He who blots out your transgressions for my own sake; and I will not remember your sins."* (Isaiah 40:25).

Forget the slander

Forget the many unkind words

Forget people who made you cry

Forget those who passed you by

Forget the pain you have silently suffered

Forget the ones who wouldn't stand by your side

When God forgives, He casts our sins in the sea of his forgetfulness and posts signs reading: ***"No Fishing."***

5. Adjust your course. The Wide World of Sports had a sports anthology series on television that ran from 1961 to 1998 and was originally hosted by Jim McKay on ABC. For years, the opening episode showed "the agony of defeat," which was a painful ending to a failed ski jump. The skier appeared to be in great form as he ran down to make the jump, but then, for no obvious reason, he would tumble end over end on the side of the jump, bouncing off the supporting structures and aborting what appeared at first to be a perfect ski jump. What viewers didn't know was that he chose to fall rather than finish the jump. Why?

As he later explained, the jump surface had become too fast, and midway down the run he realized if he completed the jump, he would land on the hard ground, beyond the safe landing area, which would have been fatal to him and perhaps endanger others as well. When the skier aborted the jump, he suffered no more than a headache from the tumble.

> *If we allow our past to quarrel with our present, we will never have a future.*

It might not be easy to adjust your course. Friends and family might not understand. It might even hurt your reputation, but change is always better than a fatal landing at the end of your run! Many of the couples I counsel tell me that they knew before they got married that they were making a mistake. However, they say they were so heavily invested in the relationship that it was difficult to break it off. What is worse: to live a life of misery or take your losses early and trust God to find a mate suitable for you?

To change the way you live, you must change the way you see yourself, as well as the way you see your circumstances.

Because of Jesus, You Have

New Potential: Many of us face the scramble for the perfect opportunity every day, always positioning ourselves for a better opportunity, a better buy, and a better promotion. Why? Because we understand that our position is essential for our future, and this is never truer than with your spiritual position. You can either be in Christ or not in Christ. Here is the good news: you don't have to scramble for it because God came looking for you to give you that new position.

The Apostle Paul wrote, "If anyone is in Christ, he is a new creation." (2 Corinthians 5:17) The new identity in Christ is mentioned more than 150 times in the New Testament. It is a radically new position for us when we find it. This is how your position will change your life:

> When you are ***not in*** Christ, you are guilty of every sin you've ever committed

When you are ***in*** Christ, you are forgiven of every sin you will ever commit

When you are ***not in*** Christ, you deserve justice
When you are ***in*** Christ, you are given grace and mercy

When you are ***not in*** Christ, you may find moments of happiness
When you are ***in*** Christ, you can find a lifetime of joy

When you are ***not in*** Christ, you seek peace in things
When you are ***in*** Christ, you have the prince of peace

New Possession: We may be able to relate to the story of the prosecuting attorney who was questioning a lady on the witness stand. He asked, *"Do you know me?"*

She answered, *"Of course, I know you. I've known you since you were a little boy. I've watched you grow up. You are a scoundrel, a heavy drinker, and a womanizer."*

The prosecuting attorney then asked, *"Do you know the attorney for the defendant?"*

"Yes," she answered, *"I sure do. I used to babysit him. I changed his diapers. I fed him his bottles. And he's grown up to be a man who is about as low as they come. He'll defend anything."*

With that, the judge called both attorneys to the bench for a side-bar. He leaned forward, looked at the two attorneys and said, *"If either of you asks this woman if she knows me, I'll hold you in contempt."*

Some of us need to rid ourselves of our old identity to allow a new one to emerge. Wouldn't you like everything to be made new in you—a new identity, a fresh start? You can have one if you are willing to allow God to give you a fresh start.

The Apostle Paul declared, "…The old has gone, the new has come!" 2Corinthians 5:17(NIV) Everything new! That is the work God brings out in our lives. New is a word God likes! One of our greatest possessions is who we are, our identity. And if we were perfectly honest, some of us need a new identity.

New Potential: "I myself no longer live, but Christ lives in me. So I live my life in this earthly body by trusting in the Son of God, who loved me and gave himself for me." Galatians 2:20 (NLT)

You have tremendous potential. Your future is better, brighter and bigger than anything in your past. For this reason, Christ's life is in you. That's potential!

When Victor Seribriakoff was 15, his teachers told him that he would never complete high school. They told him that he should drop out of school and learn a trade. Victor took the advice and, for the next 17 years, he was an itinerant doing a variety of odd jobs. He had been told he was a "dunce," so for 17 years, he lived like one. When he was 32 years old, an amazing transformation took place. An evaluation revealed that he was a genius with an I.Q. of 161. Guess what happened next? That's right, he started acting like a genius.

Since that time, he has written books, secured a number of clients, and has become a successful businessman. Perhaps the most significant event for the former high school dropout was his election as president of the International Mensa Society. Mensa has only one membership qualification: an I.Q. of 140. What was it that made the difference in Victor's life? Did he all of a sudden get smart at age 32? No, what changed was the way he saw himself.

> *It is not because things are difficult that we do not dare, it is because we do not dare that things are difficult*
>
> *Seneca*

You are a perfect 10!

There is no single factor that is more important in determining how we live than how we see ourselves and how we understand our identity. You get treated in life the way you allow people to treat you. When God created you, he put in all that you will ever need to fulfill his purpose for your life. You have gifts and talents that no one else has. On the scale of 1 to 10, 1 being the least and 10 being the greatest, you are a perfect 10 somewhere.

I heard of a hair salon called "Identity." Can you imagine the depth of emptiness that must plague people whose identity depends on their hair? Sure, our hair is important, and we need to be well-groomed, but is it really enough to completely define a person's identity? What are you basing your identity on? Many people have experienced events that have scarred their identity: abuse as a child, a failed business, a failed marriage, a failure to make the team, a moment of discretion, a sinful act. The scars are there, and they are real. Good news! When you are in Christ and when you have connected with God, He will give you a new identity and dismiss your past. With God, you have limitless potential.

When you change the way you look at things,
the things you look at will change
-Wayne Dyer

Chapter 8

Living Your Dream Life or Just Dreaming?

If all your dreams and aspirations came true, how different would your life be? Would the world be dramatically changed? Do you even have a dream?

Somewhere in the past, many us gave up on our dreams and lost touch with this essential part of our humanity. Our capacity to dream of a different us, of a more noble life, got so beaten down and repeatedly broken by people, circumstances, and disappointments that we gave up our dreams.

Often, what should be a dream that inspires us turns into a fantasy that hinders us from moving forward on the continuum from success to significance. Worse yet, we are holding on to unrealistic expectations. Have you ever met someone chasing the wrong dream? Someone obsessed with the American Idol syndrome? They are so sure of their talent and are just waiting to be discovered, but even their friends don't like to hear them sing. They remind me of a story of a young man who came to his pastor and told him that God had called upon him to preach. God, the young man said, had given him a sign by a formation of clouds that seemed to form the letters GPC. The young man took this to mean that God was telling him to "Go Preach Christ." The pastor lovingly allowed the young man to preach during the Wednesday evening service. After they heard about the message, everybody except the young man knew that he did not have the gift of preaching. The pastor came to the young man and said, Son, it looks like the letters you saw did not spell *"Go Preach Christ"* but rather, ***"Go Plant Corn."*** If you are one of those people, you may want to ask yourself, "Is this dream or just a fantasy?"

We are in dreams half-baked, half-lived, half-accomplished. We got really close and it didn't happen, so we gave up. We gave up living the life of our dreams

It is one thing to dream to be an NBA player, but unless you are at least pushing six feet, it may be a fantasy and not a dream -- unless, of course, you are a Muggsy Bogues or Earl Boykins. It may be even more so if you can't dribble, pass, or shoot. Or say you are young and aspiring to be an Olympic marathon runner, but you have an aversion to sweat and pain. Your preferences should give you a clue that this might not be the right dream for your life.

Having said that, no matter what the limitations are, it is more damaging to the human spirit to give up your dreams altogether than to try and fail. You are not a failure when you fail at something, but you are a failure when you refuse to get up and try again! I like the NBA TV commercial featuring Dwayne Wade of Miami Heat where he says, "I fall nine times. I get up ten." When your dreams are aligned with your talents, your training, your life experiences, and infused with God's enabling grace, you are in position to not only dream big, but also live large. Don't just dream. Allow God to power your imagination. When you grasp the truth that, at the core, you are a spiritual being, you begin to understand why you need God, the source of all creativity, to activate your dreams and enable you to fully live out your God-given potential.

Down through the centuries, Jesus has been the focus of discussion from theology to philosophy. His teachings on ethics and morality left an undeniable mark on world civilizations. Today, we talk of living by the golden rule, going the extra mile, or being a Good Samaritan; all concepts that we derive directly from Jesus' philosophy of life.

> *When you grasp the truth that at the core you are a spiritual being, it begins to make sense why you need God, the source of all creativity to activate your dreams and enable you to fully live out your God-given potential.*

Where we miss the point is when we don't stop to appreciate how Jesus changed the way His followers actually engaged in life. He launched a movement that defied the odds and unleashed previously untapped potential in those who believed in Him. He created a movement in which His disciples begun to believe the impossible and attempt the improbable. They soon found out that they were turning dreams into reality. His became a movement of dreamers and visionaries, called and compelled to recreate a better world.

Jesus called His followers to change the world with his message of life and love. Theirs was a life of faith and a call to expect and attempt great things for God. And, like the early disciples of Jesus, we have to dare to dream great dreams and find the courage to live them.

What Do You Want?

If you had met Christ during His earthly ministry and had the opportunity to ask Him of one thing, what would it be?

The Gospel of Mark records two conversations that are seemingly different but essentially the same. Both involve people asking Jesus for something. One of the conversations took place between Jesus and two of his close disciples—John and James. It started after Jesus disclosed to them that the time was drawing near for Him to go to Jerusalem where He would suffer, be crucified, and pay the ultimate price for our sin. However, the question that they asked Jesus showed that these words seemed to have gone right over their heads.

They came to Christ and said, "Lord, we want to you to do for us whatever we ask."

Did you ever do that to your parents when you were are child? "I want you to promise me," you'd say, which is translated to: "I want you do something for me which you might not do if you knew what it was before you promised!"

"What do you want," your parents asked you.

"Promise me first, and then I will tell you." You wanted to trick your parents to give you a "yes" answer before you disclosed the request.

Jesus asked the disciples, "What do you want?"

"When you get to your kingdom," they said, "we want to sit at your right hand and your left hand." In other words, they wanted key positions. They were preoccupied with power. They wanted to be in charge. Their thinking makes perfect sense. Jesus was king, and every king needs subjects. Jesus was going to need good trusted friends to run things for Him. James and John were early investors and wanted to secure their positions before the kingdom got too crowded. They were inciting cronyism, or looking out for your homeboy! Jesus told the disciples that those positions are not for Him to fill; besides, they didn't even know what they were asking for. In a very polite way, Jesus said to them, "Not on your life!"

There are dreams that we try to recruit God into, and sometimes I think God looks at us and, in a polite way, says, "Not on your life." God has no obligation to bless dreams that are fueled by greed, arrogance, self-indulgence, and self-centeredness. God does not say yes to everything we ask. Some of our dreams are not worth losing sleep over. Yet there are other dreams you had better not sleep on.

What is the source of your dreams? Who or what informs your dreams? How do you tell the difference between daydreaming and dreams of your soul, rooted in your desire for greatness for the glory of God?

What is Worse Than Being Blind?

Helen Keller, the first deaf and blind person to earn a bachelors' degree, was asked what she thought could be worse than being blind. Her response, was, "The only thing worse than being blind is having sight but no vision." This quote points to the key to achieving one's goals.

The second conversation that Mark recorded involved a blind man named Bartimaeus (son of Timaeus) who interrupted Jesus and his disciples (Mark 10:46-52). The healing of the blind beggar is significant in that it is the final healing that Mark reports and it appears as an interruption into the events of Jesus' Passion.

Equally bold, on the command, "Rise," Bartimaeus abandoned his sitting position as a beggar by springing up and standing like a man. Posture always gives clues to self-esteem. Never again will he be looked down upon as the scum of the earth.

Mark sets the scene when Jesus is leaving Jericho on the last leg of His journey to Jerusalem, just 15 miles away. Passover was approaching and the road was jam packed with pilgrims chanting on the way to the Holy City. Alongside the road was another crowd—parade watchers, curiosity seekers, and those who were too poor, sinful, diseased, or handicapped to make the journey to Jerusalem. By now, the size of the crowd following after Jesus had swelled to "a great multitude" (v. 46).

Moving people together in a festival atmosphere must have filled the air with a tingle of triumph. After all, the news that the young rabbi who, for three years, had challenged the religious establishment of the Jews was on His way to Jerusalem for the final showdown with religious authorities created a lot of excitement. After all, the promise of a confrontation always draws a crowd.

Amid the cacophony of sound, a disrupting voice pierced through the noise and called, "Jesus, Son of David, have mercy on me!" (v. 47) Some of the people tried yelling at him as they always did, telling him to stop being a public nuisance. However, the blind man could see something that no one else could see and cried all the more, "Son of David, have mercy on me!"

Both the plaintive sound and the prophetic greeting of Bartimaeus stopped Jesus in His tracks. Presumably, His healing ministry had concluded and all of His energy now had to be marshaled for His own suffering. Nothing could deter or interrupt Him except a needy man crying for mercy.

When Jesus heard his cry, He stopped and called for him. The summons, "be of good cheer" appealed to emotions Bartimaeus thought were gone forever. Perhaps, he had heard "cheer up" before from callous, insincere people who tossed a coin in his begging blanket. Never before had he heard words of encouragement combined with the command, "Rise." A serious call to faith required an act of will, as well as a word of hope.

Crowds are fickle. The same crowd who tried to silence him was now calling him when they realized Jesus was on His side. The information that "He is calling you" tested the level of Bartimaeus's cognitive skills.

Look Up, Get Up and Go

In his past, no one had ever responded to his call, except to push him down and demand silence to put him in his place, one of obscurity. Perhaps even then, the beggar must have thought that a cruel hoax was in the making. Raw intelligence and refined intuition, however, told Bartimaeus the truth. As a blind beggar, he had no place to go but up. The risk was minimal. As simple as it seems, the call to "look up, get up, and go up" defines faith as an act of hope based upon limited information. The blind man did not have much information to work with. All he had was a few words of encouragement from people who were, just minutes earlier, his harshest critics.

I wonder what would happen if we started acting on what we know God has already told us to do. We may not have all the information, but that should not stop us from acting on what we know God wants us to do or who He wants us to become.

If ever a person enthusiastically demonstrated a holistic show of faith, Bartimaeus did. Feeling for feeling, will for will, mind for mind, he answered the call from Jesus. In response to the word of encouragement, "Be of good cheer" (v. 49), he went a step further and, in a daring act, threw aside the ragged garment that served functionally to catch coins and symbolically stood as a sign of his lowly lifestyle as a beggar. Equally bold, on the command, "Rise," he abandoned his sitting position as a beggar by springing up and standing like a man. Posture always gives clues to self-esteem. Never again would Bartimaeus be looked down upon as the scum of the earth. Just as Job responded to God's challenge, Bartimaeus stood ready to answer as a man.

Claim Your Big Dream

To complete his show of faith, Bartimaeus came to Jesus. All of his life, the blind beggar had counted on others to lead and feed him. Although still blind, Bartimaeus walked out to claim his big dream—the dream to have sight. What a sight it must have been to see the crowd open a path for Bartimaeus as he walked to Jesus! *In one sense, faith had already made him a whole man. His feelings, his will, and his mind were healed.*

Jesus met the ready faith of Bartimaeus with the open-ended question, "What do you want me to do for you?" Now, that's a strange question. In the first place, Jesus is God, and He ought to know what the blind man needs. In any case, even if He weren't God, it would require little imagination to figure out what a blind beggar wants! It's not like He was going to say "Lord, I would like to hear better to compensate for my blindness." Or "Lord, increase my intuition and heighten my senses so I do not have to run into objects as I grope in the dark." Better yet, he was not going to say, "Lord, you know when I obeyed your command and got up, I was so excited I threw away my coat and my begging bow, so can you give me a warmer blanket and a better begging bow?"

The difference between Bartimaeus answer and the Disciples request is the difference between faith and ambition. Faith asks for needs, ambition begs for wants

Instead, you have to admire the blind man's bold request. "Teacher," the blind man said, "I want to see."

Jesus responded, "Go your way; your faith has healed you." Instantly, the blind man could see, and he followed Jesus down the road.

Not long before this incident, James and John had asked Jesus to grant them whatever they asked. The difference between Bartimaeus' answer and the disciples' request is the difference between faith and ambition. Faith asks for needs; ambition begs for wants. Bartimaeus needed his sight; James and John wanted the places of honor in the coming kingdom of God.

Jesus exempted Himself from responding to the disciples' wants, but He wasted no time in meeting Bartimaeus' need. The phrase "go your way; your faith has made you well" (v. 52) not only gives instant sight to a blind man, but also recognizes the total healing of a person with a ready faith. *Spiritually free, physically sound, and humanly dignified, Bartimaeus is declared "well" and "whole."*

Mark reinforces the total healing of Bartimaeus by bringing the story full cycle in the conclusion, "And immediately, he received his sight and followed Jesus on the road." (v. 52) A beggar becomes a disciple. A squatter becomes a dignified pilgrim—seeing, living, walking, and singing proof that Jesus is Savior and Lord.

What is driving you? If you were that blind man, would you have given the same answer that the blind man gave? Would you start with your deepest longing, the dream that seems too good to be true?

Your dreams are the product of your longings. The dreams that fuel your life are fueled by your desires, your passions, and your cravings. They are the things that burn inside you that you need to achieve in order to live your complete life.

Ask for Sight in Both Eyes

Many of us are like Bartimaeus except we are going to God saying, "Lord, will you give me sight in one eye?" instead of boldly asking, "Lord, could you give me 20/20 vision? I want to see; I want clarity in my life." It is possible that you are not living the life of your dreams because God has asked you what you want, and you desire far too little. Have you been willing to settle for far much less than your dreams?

I think much of our praying makes God wonder why we think so little of Him. I can just imagine God looking at us and asking,

"What do you want?" And when we answer, He shakes His head and thinks, *if I could just get you to believe more, to care more, to want more than you are asking for!*

Chapter 9

Dream Busters

Another story in the Bible records the life of a young man called Joseph. If you are familiar with Broadway, you know Joseph. He is the guy with the multicolored coat, walking around with a bit of showmanship. He was metro way before metro was fashionable. In Genesis 37, we are introduced to Joseph's character:

> Joseph was a young man, seventeen years old. He and his brothers, the sons of Bilhah and Zilpah, his father's wives, cared for the flocks. Joseph gave his father bad reports about his brothers. Since Joseph was born when his father Israel was old, Israel loved him more than his other sons. He made Joseph a special robe with long sleeves. When Joseph's brothers saw that their father loved him more than he loved them, they hated their brother and could not speak to him politely. One time, Joseph had a dream, and when he told his brothers about it, they hated him even more. Joseph said, "Listen to the dream I had. We were in the field tying bundles of wheat together. My bundle stood up, and your bundles of wheat gathered around it and bowed down to it." His brothers said, "Do you really think you will be king over us?

Do you truly think you will rule over us?" His brothers hated him even more because of his dreams and what he had said. Then Joseph had another dream, and he told his brothers about it also. He said, "Listen, I had another dream. I saw the sun, moon, and eleven stars bowing down to me."

If God gives you a dream, it will come to pass if you courageously choose to pursue it, not because you become a salesman for it.

Evidently, Joseph had not read the book on how to make friends and influence people. Not only was he a spoiled brat, but he was also a bit of a snitch. The brothers hated the fact that their father gave him a coat of many colors. To add insult to injury, he snitched on them and then had dreams that made him the center of their universe!

Here is some advice: even if you are pursuing a dream given to you by God, don't go around telling everybody! There are dream busters out there, waiting to abort your dreams. If God gives you are dream for your life's purpose, it will come to pass if you choose to courageously pursue it, but not because you became a salesman for it. To be sure, you have two kinds of dreams. There are going up dreams and giving up dreams. If yours is a giving up dream, by all means, share it with your friends. If you want to give up a bad habit or lose weight, tell that to as many people as you have in your circle of friendship. They will hold you accountable. However, if it is a going up dream—you want to be the best student in your class, or you want to build the most successful business in your industry—keep that to yourself.

God gives God-sized dreams to people with a God-sized capacity to believe Him. I think Joseph made a huge mistake to share his dreams with his brothers. His immaturity created a relational rift and caused unnecessary sibling rivalry. However, that did not derail God's plan for Joseph's life. While his brothers despised him and tried everything they knew to stop him, God won in the end.

The process in Joseph's life took not days or months, or even years, but decades. This should be an encouragement to those of us who may grow discouraged that our efforts are not being rewarded and to those of us who panic because we believe we are fast approaching the end of our runway but our plane is not lifting!

Sometimes the life God desires for us takes a lifetime to come to pass. Great lives that are born of great dreams often come through great sacrifice and great suffering. And, at the heart of the issue, perhaps it is not how long it takes for the dream to come to pass but how long it takes God to make the dreamer.

Your dreams are the result of your longings, a portrait of your potential, and a promise for your future.[34] Your dreams are God's way of gently speaking to your heart and saying, *"There is more to you than you know. There is more available to you than you can imagine. I want to give you more than you are asking for. There is an extraordinary life awaiting you if you would only trust me."*

Are You Ready to Live?

There were times in the life of the Israelites when it looked like all hope had gone. They believed in God, but they didn't believe He could fix their problems. Have you ever been there? Have you experienced those low points in your life where you believed in God, believed in the Bible, increased your religious activity, but your life was still a mess? You say to yourself, I am a shipwreck. I have blown it. I

[34] McManus, p. 22

have absolutely destroyed my potential for ever living the life of my dreams.

Speak to the Wind

At such moments, your dreams might best be described as nothing but dead, dry bones. You are just waiting to be put six feet under. On your tombstone, you may as well write: Died at 25, Buried at 70. And it may be that God is asking you a question, just like he asked Ezekiel the prophet centuries ago:

> *Then He asked me, "Human, can these bones live?"*
>
> *I answered, "Lord GOD, only you know."*
>
> *He said to me, "Prophesy to these bones and say to them, 'Dry bones, hear the word of the LORD. This is what the Lord GOD says to the bones: I will cause breath to enter you so you will come to life. I will put muscles on you and flesh on you and cover you with skin. Then I will put breath in you so you will come to life. Then you will know that I am the LORD...Then he said to me, "Prophesy to the wind. Proph-*

esy, human, and say to the wind, 'This is what the Lord GOD says: Wind, come from the four winds, and breathe on these people who were killed so they can come back to life.' So I prophesied as the LORD commanded me. And the breath came into them, and they came to life and stood on their feet, a very large army.

(Ezekiel 37: 1-10 NCV)

I think most of us have a life that is like Ezekiel's valley of dry bones—lifeless, scattered, and dry. Maybe you have blown it countless times. You have promised yourself and said to God, "This time, I am going to get it right. I am serious. I am going to get it done." However, as soon as you come out of the gate, you come crashing down, and in your mind you are nothing but dry, old bones. You can't even find your way to the grave.

God wants to ask you one more time, "Can these bones live again?" Then he follows that by asking you to do the impossible. "Speak to the winds and say, 'This is what the almighty God says: Come O breath, from the four winds.'"

"Right," you think, "speak to the winds. Sure. Every day the wind does my biding. It's truly amazing to see the wind follow my commands. God, you must be kidding! I never controlled one breath of wind. Now you are asking me to command all four?"

God often asks for us to believe or do what we think is the impossible. However, if you do His bidding, no matter how impossible or strange it seems, you will find yourself experiencing unexpected or miraculous results.

Head Games

What most impossible situation are you facing? What fears threaten you? What darkness has consumed you and drained your vitality, sucked out your soul, and left your dreams lying lifeless in the valley of despair?

> ***Failure can become as state of being, as can despair!***

Re-writing our life script must begin by changing our minds as well as our actions. Thus, we must begin by engaging in a fundamentally new plot and a storyline. Life will appear to us in ways we see and believe it to be. Our beliefs inform us and drive our behavior. Behavior drives performance. Repeated performance forms character, and character determines our final destiny.

In a classic study, the audience was asked to observe people dribbling and passing a basketball. The instruction: to count the number of times each person caught and passed the ball in the space of one minute. Intense concentration was needed because the ball moved quickly. At the height of activity, someone dressed in a gorilla suit crossed the floor, walked between the players, turned, beat his chest, and then left. How many people saw such a phenomena? Harvard graduates and recipients of the Nobel Prize in Psychology Daniel Simons and Christopher Chabris found that, consistently, 50% of the people failed to notice the gorilla.[35]

This "inattention blindness" is our brain at work trying to make sense and construct meaning and consistent narratives from an inconsistent world. Things that don't neatly fit the storyline are unconsciously ed-

[35] Christopher Chabris and Daniel Simons met at Harvard University in 1997, where they began to collaborate on research. In 2004, they received the Nobel Prize in Psychology, awarded for "achievements that first make people laugh, and then make them think," for the experiment that inspired The Invisible Gorilla. Their scholarly research focuses on the limits of human perception, memory, and awareness, and is best known for showing that people are far less aware of their visual surroundings than they think.

ited out, or simply fail to register all together. In the end, we become comfortable and dependent on our old habits informed by previously accepted data. Uncertainty and discomfort arises when we begin to move from existing internal models.

How does Ezekiel make sense of all this? As a Jew, Ezekiel believed in the resurrection in the eschaton (the last day), but not just yet. What may appear to be lifeless ideas and long forgotten dreams may well hold the key to your life of adventure, a heroic life, void of monotony, teeming with danger, adventure and the unknown, but also holding the greatest promise of fulfillment.

> *"A man is but the product of his thoughts*
> *what he thinks, he becomes."*
> *Mahatma Gandhi*

Maybe there is a dream buried deep in your heart, and God is waiting to resurrect it, to put all the bones back together. He is waiting to put flesh, muscle, and sinew on it and wrap skin around it. Like Ezekiel, you may still believe your dream will come true but, in the back of your mind, you are convinced that it is not time yet.

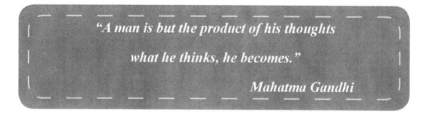

God knows you cannot control the wind, but He can. If He commands you to act and you obey, you will see all creation moving in concert to accomplish with you what you were created to do. Long before you were born, you were a dream in God's mind. He saw your potential, and He alone knows the full extent of your creative genius.

CHAPTER 10

Co-Creators with God

The Genesis account of the origins of our planet makes a simple but deeply profound statement in regard to the creation of man. Scripture opens with this simple declaration:

> *"Then God said, 'Let us make human beings* ***in our image and likeness****. And let them rule over the fish in the sea and the birds in the sky, over the tame animals, over all the earth, and over all the small crawling animals on the earth.' So God created human beings in His image. In the image of God, He created them. He created them male and female. God blessed them and said, 'Have many children and grow in number. Fill the earth and be its master. Rule over the fish in the sea and over the birds in the sky and over every living thing that moves on the earth.'"*
>
> (Gen 1:26-28)

Theologians have not done too well in recent years in the ongoing dialogue with scientific inquiry with regard to creation. And while questions still abound as to how and how long, the Bible sheds sufficient light as to the "who" of creation—God. As a theologian, one particular approach that has made me uneasy is the approach that forces a believer to be totally immersed in Scripture like a hippopotamus in a river, emerging only to snort at the latest discoveries that are considered as irreverent or misleading science.

Many times, the impossible is simply the untried.

The problem with this attitude is that it suggests that all that man needs to know about life can be found in the Bible, and everything discovered from other sources is, at best, irrelevant and, at worst, devilish. I remember a time in seminary when a speaker gave a lecture series on creation and made the unyielding assertion that ours is a very young earth—no older than 4,000-6,000 years. It should come as no surprise that many Christians still hold on to this "young earth" view despite *evidence from radiometric age dating of meteorite material* that points to a much older earth. To be sure, the evolutionary argument is impossible with a young earth.

I do not wish to delve into that debate. For the purpose of this book, I will, however, point out that there are two words that describe God's creative activity—*"progression"* and *"power."* The Hebrew words *tōhū wābōhû,* translated to the phrase *"without form and void,"* call our attention on the condition of creation in its initial stages.

The fact that God created something ex nihilo (a Latin term meaning *"out of nothing"*), while not explicitly stated, is continually implied throughout Scripture, even as seen in the Apostle Paul's statement about God *"who gives life to the dead and calls into existence the things that do not exist."* (Rom. 4:17, RSV) Without question, creation progressed from a state of *"nothingness"* through a state of *"formlessness"* and *"emptiness"* to a condition where the *"formlessness"* gave way to *"form"* and the *"emptiness"* gave way to *"fullness."*

God's grace, expressed in the daily supply of our basic needs, also gives us freedom to imagine, to innovate, to create. Our capacity to create derived from his image in us is limitless

Furthermore, we are told that God created man in His own image. Whatever else that means, I believe it means that we are co-creators with God. For some, it may be scandalous—even sacrilegious—to think that we are a part of God's ongoing creative process. We would rather sit back and be content with the idea that only God begins and completes the creative process. After all, He is the master artist, the creator of heaven and earth. He is just that much better than any of us. I fully agree, but that's not the way God set it to work. The Creator has the ultimate power to create but has also invited us to join Him in the ongoing creative process.

You are created to create. That's your birthright. That's your destiny. To create is your essence, and it's crucial for living the life God intended. For many years, I walked around with the false belief that I was not creative. I convinced myself that I had no originality; I was not innovative, and I couldn't create. When I was in the 11th grade, we were asked to write poems in Kiswahili. I think the class was "fasihi" or something like that. Or maybe that is what a poem is called in Kiswahili. Either way, I hated it. I wrote my poem in protest and, when it was time for me to share my creativity with my classmates, I proudly walked in front of the class and read my poem:

Shahiri safari nenda
Hadi Uganda, Rwuanda
Kisha Burundi urudi

Then I announced, "That's it!" My non-poem became the joke of the year. I was proud that I had finally convinced my teacher and my fellow students that I was not creative. In other words, I was saying in essence, "Guys, when it comes to creativity, do not bother me. Just leave me alone. Go on and become innovators, creators and originators. I will just walk behind you and synthesize your ideas and copy your ingenuity."

> *"All the World's a Stage, and all the men and women merely players."*
>
> *Shakespeare*

I have deep suspicion that I am not alone in this line of thinking. Many people have resigned themselves to the idea that they are not creative. They are just happy to participate in other people's thoughts, ideas, and innovation. They are happy to live with the limitations imposed on them by their upbringing, their life experiences, and their past relationships and failures. However, this is a big lie.

Shakespeare wrote "All the world's a stage, and all the men and women merely players." Do you agree with Shakespeare? Do you like the play you are acting in right now? Are you happy with your role, your lines, and your characters? Would you like to rewrite the script? You can take the lead role, but often you may give the starring part to others. This can be good because there are times when stepping back and letting others have center stage is a kind, caring gesture. Anyone hogging the limelight all the time would be selfish and attention seeking. However, that is not to say that you have to live by the script handed to you by circumstances.

Sometimes we think that if we strike out by faith and leave everything we know, it's going to get worse from here. However, it is likely that you'll never find greater contentment or joy until you are willing to give up what you know for what awaits and exists in the unknown. To be sure, we often do not get to choose the context from which our life begins or the role handed to us by society. We don't get to choose our parents, our race, or our ethnicity. We don't get to choose our economic condition when we are born into this world. We absolutely have no say about the beginning of our life's journey, but we have a great deal to say about the destination of our journey and how that journey shapes us day by day. The good news is there are still many ideas out there to be explored.

Creating the Unlimited with the Limited

Have you ever listened to music and wondered if there would be a day when new lyrics were not created? Suppose one day, we all woke up to find that every melody had been written, every lyric penned, and every note expressed. From that day on, everything would be retro because every form of music had been explored. It would become as Solomon said in the book of Ecclesiastes, "vanity of vanities, nothing is new under the sun."

However, the "all is vanity" verdict is only true when life is viewed from man's limited perspective under the sun. Vanity marks the limits of our ability to understand and change the way life works. It mocks in its gloomy way the sovereignty of God whose mysteries are to us unfathomable, as we are too profound to fully explore. When it comes to the future, our lives are more discovered than predetermined. However, to create that life, we are going to need to risk all. At times, it will require us to move in a direction that is not even clear and in areas that are not fully scripted.

I wish the moment we enter into a relationship with God, the Holy Spirit would send us daily memos that spell out everything in detail.

That would be easy but not as exciting. Instead, we find that life is not a color-within-the-lines kindergarten project. You have to keep mixing colors, creating new blends, and seeing things in fresh ways. There are times where you will get paint all over you because life is about growth. Growth not only demands change, but can also be messy and because of that, demands humility.

The life that God offers gives us an alternative conclusion than the "all is vanity" verdict. It is a life filled with joy that brings relief in the midst of frustration. It announces that God's puzzling clouds of sovereignty carry a silver lining of grace. His grace, expressed in the daily supply of our basic needs, also gives us freedom to imagine, to innovate, to adapt, and to create. Our capacity to create is limitless and infinite.

Twelve Notes

It is amazing that there are so many sounds, songs, and styles of music, especially when you consider the inherent limitation: there are only 12 notes. Out of these 12 notes, generation after generation, culture after culture, year after year, we are still coming up with ways to express new sounds—jazz, rap, hip-hop, punk, classical, disco, reggae, techno, R&B, alternative, rumba, scratching, opera, twist, blue grass, country, and the beat goes on and on. One would think that we should have exhausted those 12 notes by now. And yet when you visit India, or Japan, or the Philippines, or Brazil, or Mexico, or New Zealand or Kenya, those same notes are expressed in culturally rich, diverse ways.

Three Primary Colors

The same concept applies to the field of art. You would expect that, at some point, there would be no more original paintings; after all, there are only three primary colors: red, blue and green. That's it! What can you really do with only three colors? And you thought 12 notes were a limitation, artists could say. Three colors, talk about your hands being tied in the innovative process. Do not tell that to artists, though. They live in a world of ever expanding horizons—no boundaries, no parameters, and no limitations.

Just visit your local art museum and see creativity on display. Human beings have been painting since pre-historic times. An example of an early painting dated between 30,000 B.C. and 28,000 B.C. was found in Chauvet Cave, in Vallon-Pont-dArc, Ardeche, France. Even after the impressionists Van Gogh and Claude Monet, or the abstract cubist Pablo Picasso, or modern day digital artist, new forms of art are still being created—all from three primary colors!

Lines, Circles and Angles

In the field of architecture, all they have are lines, circles, and angles. Architects do not have much to work with—just those same three shapes. That's it. One would think that some architect would be the last to design the original building, but they keep springing up one after another, city after city, from country to country. It comes down to how you arrange those lines, circles and lines.

Nine Digits

The last time I took a math class, I was told that there are only nine digits. I do not think much has changed since, despite protests by mathematicians that the discovery of zero changed everything. Regardless, from these nine digits, you have an infinite number of configurations and possibilities. With only nine digits, Astronomers have spied galaxies 12.3 billion light years from the earth!

To put that in perspective, in grade school, we were taught that light traveling at 186,000 miles per second only takes 8 minutes to travel the 93 million miles between the sun and our planet. Think about that. Sunlight is only 8 minutes old. However, light from the furthest galaxy takes 12.3 billion light years to get to us. I cannot get my mind around that concept, can you? The field of mathematics is proof that things that appear to limit us in actuality have limitless possibilities. Even though we have a finite number of materials and parameters that hem our lives in, we are only limited by the extent of our imagination. Starting with only nine digits, scientists can calculate not only the furthest distances, but also the shortest distance and time. The shortest possible time, we are told, is 10^{-43} seconds. In quantum mechanics, this is called Planck Time. Any time shorter than this, and quantum mechanics cannot tell whether events are simultaneous or sequential. Similarly, the shortest possible distance is 1.6×10^{-35} meters. This is called Planck Length. Any distance shorter than that and quantum mechanics cannot distinguish between here and there or anywhere, for that matter.[36] The next time you catch yourself drifting into thinking that you have tried everything and nothing seems to work, just think about the inherent limitations that the human race has overcome.

[36] God can do far more than just relieve your tension headaches and help you go to sleep. More than regulating your nightmarish life, He wants to work with you to create a future far brighter than you've ever imagine. And here is the good news: you already have everything you need.

It is sad that, when it comes to life, we accept the notion that all that is left is for us to be clones of one another. We are content to be carbon copies of others people's innovation. We have bought into the notion that we are incapable of creating. As children, we were blessed with the gift of curiosity. Just as God created you to dream, to imagine, and to design, He also created you to learn, to grow and to invent. However, as it were, one of the casualties in our journey to adulthood is the unique gift of curiosity. You do not have to tell a child to look, to explore, to feel, or to eat. You do not have to teach children to be curious. Every child is born and infused with a strong dose of curiosity—insatiably curious, dangerously curious, maybe even irritatingly curious.

"If I were to wish for something, I would wish not for wealth or power but for the passion of possibility, for the eye, eternally young, eternally ardent, that sees possibility everywhere."

Søren Kierkegaard

"Curiosity," wrote McManus, "unfortunately is far too often relegated to the place of a childhood luxury. Our passion for discovery and exploration becomes another victim of growing up."[37] When we lose our imagination, we put our curiosity to rest. We call this "being honest with ourselves." We don't want to live dangerously. After all, curiosity killed the cat, and we are trying to survive. We just want to make it. Maybe in the past, you really did not get positive results from your curiosity. It didn't kill you, but it came close and left you significantly emotionally injured. You took your chances with relationships, business ventures, or whatever the risk, and you got burned. So, you gave up your insatiable curiosity in exchange for comfort, security, and predictability. Now, your best line is "once bitten twice shy" or "better safe than sorry." In effect, you have reduced your existence to risk management.

God can do far more than just relieve your tension headaches and help you go to sleep. More than regulating your nightmarish life, He wants to work with you to create a future far brighter than you've ever imagine. And here is the good news- you already have everything you need.

[37] McManus, p. 35

However, if you are going to experience the life God has designed for you, you are going to have to once again choose to explore, to imagine and to create. You have to begin taking calculated risks. You have to start making yourself flexible and pliable again, because if you stop growing, you will never experience a life beyond the one you have right now. God created us with an unlimited capacity to learn.

In the Genesis account, Adam was tasked with the responsibility of naming all the animals; whatever he called them, that's what they were. Creation was raw and unshaped, and God expected Adam to work with Him to complete the process. Sometimes, I wonder what would have happened if Adam had stopped at the 100th animal. There would have been perhaps thousands of nameless animals! Now that doesn't mean that you can learn everything there is out there to know, but it does mean that you can learn everything there is for you to achieve your dreams.

. . . By the way, all you need is just one more solution than you have problems!

God has also given us the ability to know our limitations. At my age,

I doubt that I can be a space scientist or a molecular physicist. There are inherent limitations to those ambitions, but that doesn't mean I am doomed in my present condition. If a wall is a limitation, how smart do you have to be to know that a wall is there? Once you bang your head on the wall two or three times, you might conclude, "There is a wall here." Real genius, real invention, is not in identifying the problem but in finding solutions. Problems, obstacles and challenges can either become permanent markers of your limitations, or they can become the stepping-stones into a whole new world. By the way, all you need is just one more solution than you have problems. Getting that one more solution begins with your willingness to take calculated risks and use your innovation to create the life you desire.

Unleash Your Own Becoming

Often, creativity is the misunderstood child of the genius family. We convince ourselves that we are not creative because we are not one of those genius "geeks." I like the commercial from the sports drink Gatorade that asks, "Is it in you?" Truthfully, the answer is yes, and here is the good news: you don't need anyone's affirmation.

In *The Fountainhead*, a 1943 novel by Ayn Rand, there is an interesting story about creativity. Howard Roark, the protagonist in the novel, is depicted as an individualistic young architect who chooses to struggle in obscurity rather than compromise his artistic and personal vision. Roark, a young, aspiring architect, firmly believes that a person must be a "prime mover" to achieve pure art, not mitigated by others, as opposed to councils or committees of individuals which lead to compromise and mediocrity and a "watering down" of a prime mover's compelling vision. He represents the triumph of individualism over the slow stagnation of collectivism. Bowing to no one, Roark rises from an unknown architect who was kicked out of school for "drawing outside of the lines."

Roark goes on to design many landmark buildings and rails against conventional wisdom. He is eventually arrested and brought to trial for dynamiting a building he designed, whose design was compromised by other architects brought in to give a second opinion and negate his singular vision of the project. During his trial, Roark delivers a speech condemning "second-handers" and declaring the superiority of prime movers. He prevails and is vindicated by the jury. On one occasion, while defending his creativity, he said:

"Thousands of years ago, the first man discovered how to make fire. He was probably burned at the stake he had taught his brothers to light. He was considered an evildoer who had dealt with a demon mankind dreaded. But thereafter, men had fire to keep them warm, to cook their food, to light their caves. He had left them a gift they had not conceived and he had lifted darkness from the earth. Centuries later, the first man invented the wheel. He was probably torn on the rack he had taught his brothers to build. He was considered a transgressor who ventured into forbidden territory. But thereafter, men could travel passed any horizon. He had left them a gift they had not conceived and he had opened the roads of the world."[38]

That man, that solitary individual, that un-submissive and first, stands in the opening chapter of every major turning point known to mankind. Through the centuries, there were men who dared to take the first step down new and uncharted roads, armed with nothing but their own vision. Their goals and aspirations differed, but they all had this

[38] Rand, Ayn, The Fountainhead (Archibald Ogden, NY 1948), 710

one thing in common: *their step was first, the road new, the vision un-borrowed, and the response they received—ridicule!* The great creators—the thinkers, the artists, the scientist, the pioneer missionaries, and the inventors—all stood alone against the men of their age. Every great new invention was met with rejection. The first motor was considered foolish. The airplane was considered impossible. The power loom was considered vicious. Anesthesia was considered sinful. *Still, the men of raw and un-borrowed vision pressed on. They fought, they suffered, they endured loneliness, and they paid the price. In the end, they won.* Today, we are better for their struggles. That first man drew inspiration from himself and much grace was given him by God.

> ***Man cannot survive except through being creative.***
> ***He comes on earth a weakling, unarmed.***
> ***His brain is his only weapon.***

Man cannot survive except through being creative. He comes on earth a weakling, unarmed. His brain is his only weapon. Animals obtain their food by force. Man has no claws, no fangs, no horns (though I have met few people who think they do have horns), and no great strength to muscle his way through life. He must plant his food, or hunt it, or buy it. To plant, he needs to map his plot, and then use tools to nurture his garden. To hunt, he needs weapons; and to make weapons, a process of thought. To buy, he must work. To work, he must get an education, acquire a skill or learn a trade. From the simplest necessity to the highest scientific abstraction, from the wheel to the newest jet fighter, everything we are and everything we have comes from a single attribute of man—the function of his reasoning mind. So why are we not as creative? The truth is, we have allowed mental blockades to prevent us from becoming everything we were created to be.

The signature of mediocrity is not the unwillingness to change but a refusal to let go of the obvious

If we choose, we can become more aware of the blocks that hinder our creativity, thus becoming more connected, more enthusiastic, and more focused on our spiritual and professional growth. Here are simple steps you can take to unleash your own becoming. Each step has a corresponding creativity trap, or obstacle, that must be overcome in order to move forward:

Step One: Take out the Trash! Like our homes that are filled with gadgets, tools, and just pain garbage that we no longer use or need, our minds are cluttered with ideas and beliefs we once thought were useful but are, in reality, clogging our creativity. We have not used those ideas or implemented those projects for a long time but they still clog our brain. Clutter around the home ends up taking up useful space and restricts our movement, as do self-defeating ideas.

Obstacle to Step one: Toleration. Toleration produces mediocrity. A "toleration" is something or some habit you have been putting up with for a long time. You have had some stuff on your to-do list for months or even years. We often do not know that the thing in our way is "toleration" because we have put up with it for so long that it becomes second nature. At some point, we have to draw a line in the sand and say enough is enough. I am not putting up with this anymore.

Step Two: Clarity. Create a clear and compelling picture of the future you desire, keeping in mind that life does not give you what you desire, but what you demand. You must move beyond desire to put a demand on life. Whatever your heart's desire, begin now by narrowing down the specific steps you need to take. Being specific is the key.

If we are expecting God to support our new idea, we must make our "recipe" as specific as possible. Imagine your child asking you to help prepare breakfast although the child has not decided whether to eat scrambled eggs, omelet, grits, or just plain cereal. Be specific.

Obstacle to Step Two: Perfectionism. In 2003, I was invited to be a founding board member of a Kenyan organization based in Atlanta—The Association of Kenyan Professionals in Atlanta (AKPA). One day, I proudly announced to the board members that "I am a victim of my own perfectionism." By this I meant, when it comes to assignments, I would not consider taking any board assignment unless I was certain I could do it to perfection. I thought I was being cute, but I was being just plain stupid. When I look back, that is one of the organizations in which my contribution was little to none. I started with a handicap—the belief that I had to execute my responsibility to perfection. Excellence does not always mean perfection. I have since come to have a more realistic view of myself. I am human, and all I can do is use the best opportunities I have available to me. I don't have to wait until the exact right moment. Besides, any mistakes I make along the way are a gift.

Step Three: Collaboration. Some creative ideas are so huge that you need support and reinforcement. Putting a team of supporting cast around you can mean the difference between getting your breakthrough or falling flat on your face because you didn't have enough support. Asking for support around your creative ideas invites intimacy and demands that you make yourself vulnerable.

Obstacle to Step Three: Unhealthy Boundaries. Your personal time and space is sacred. Do not allow your boundaries to become so porous that you allow people to take up your time, energy, and space to the extent that you cannot execute your plans. You know who they are—those friends, family members, and coworkers who drain your energy. Learn to say "NO." Telling someone upfront that you only have so much time to give to them is much easier than sitting through another boring lunch hour with Bubba. That's time you could spend working toward your goals.

Step Four: Confidence. President Barak Obama built his grassroots movement that took the world by a storm on a simple motto: ***"Yes, we can."*** During his second run that, by all estimates, looked improbable, he narrowed his campaign slogan to one word: ***"FORWARD."*** If you know anything about the depth of racist sentiments in the United States, you will appreciate the confidence it took for a skinny young man born of a Kenyan father and a white mother from Kansas to even entertain the idea that he could be president of the United States.

The number one confidence and trust booster is keeping your agreements. Increased confidence is a natural by-product of keeping agreements with yourself and others. Your life stands or falls by how well you keep agreements. Do what you say you are going to do. Start by being on time with your agreements and see how that gives you a fulfilling feeling and inspires you to do more. However, don't take my word for it; try it out! Give yourself the test of being everywhere you have agreed to be 15 minutes early for three weeks and see if you don't feel more confident. People will want to do business with you too. I guarantee it.

Obstacle to step Four: Resentment and Jealousy. Being in Christian ministry, I have seen these twin traps work effectively to stop the flow of creativity in many pastors. Pastor "A" sees pastor "B" prospering even though he cannot preach himself out of a paper bag. He begins to resent the fact that pastor "B" is prospering despite his suspicious theology. If this continues, the unique character and calling of Pastor A will never emerge because he is not looking at himself. His focus is on someone else's ability. Jealousy and resentment are showstoppers. These are huge "creativity blockers."

Step Five: Connection. Creativity occurs when your heart and mind connect to someone or something (an idea, a solution). This passion provides further inspiration and expands the joy of innovation. Find a way to connect to your creative idea at the heart level. Once you find inspiration, you will be creating in no time, and your joy will abound.

Obstacle to Step Five: Distractions and Addictions. What is your number one distraction? To some, it is computer games, television, social media, or talking on the phone. These are precious time and energy stealers we allow when we don't want to engage in creative thinking. I am not suggesting you give up television or social media altogether. All you need to do is to keep a watchful eye to make sure you are staying on task. Allocate the best time of the day to be the time to think creatively and shape your thoughts until a winning idea forms in your mind.

Chapter 11

Harness the Power of Focus

In the spring of 1986, I had coveted the opportunity to travel to the United States for the first time. I was in my mid-twenties and, by this time, I had traveled to other countries like Singapore, India, Pakistan, the Netherlands, Egypt, Ethiopia, Malawi, and Zambia. Every time I returned home, I brought back fascinating stories of my experiences in ministry and insightful discoveries of other cultures. For the first time, I discovered that even though we humans all have the same basic needs (food, shelter, clothing), our culture informs us what is acceptable and what is not. In Singapore, for example, I enjoyed what tasted like chicken all week until we went to the meat market to stock up on our supply and, to my utter amazement, they were selling snakes by the foot! To be sure, snake tastes like chicken.

The focus of your life should not be your shortcomings, your failures, sin, guilt or shame.

So I left Kenya armed with a new Nikon camera and rolls of film to document my visit. I was anxious to share my memories with friends and relatives upon my return to Kenya. In the United States, I took hundreds of pictures of historic sites, including the Washington Monument, the Smithsonian, and the State Capitol. We traveled from Washington D.C. by bus to Atlanta, Georgia, and made many stops along the way. On every stop, I made sure I took pictures of wonderful memories with friends and hosts from Singapore, the Philippines, Indonesia, Pakistan, Sudan, and Malawi. On one occasion, we stopped for lunch, and my friend from Indonesia ordered hotdogs. My friend made a scene when his order came and it was not what he expected. "I said dog. I want the real dog," he demanded. The waitress kindly told him that they don't serve dog meat in the United States. "No," he insisted, "but you have it right here on your menu." I caught these memories and many other cross-cultural miscues like it with my camera. This was going to be a trip to treasure for the rest of my life; I was going to make my parents proud to see how their son from humble beginnings was now preaching on the world stage.

After two months of travel and hundreds of pictures, I flew back to Kenya, excited to go home. However, when I went to pick my pictures from the photo shop, I discovered that the unthinkable had happened. As soon as I walked into the photo shop, I could tell something was not right from the look on the face of the gentleman who greeted me.

With a heavy Indian accent, the guy said, "I am very, very, sorry, sir; you have no pictures."

"Why?" I protested with a mixture of disbelief, frustration, and anger.

"Well, sir," he explained, "it seems like your camera was out of focus the entire time you took your pictures. So nothing developed."

Apparently, I had not learned how to use the camera enough to know how to adjust the lens. It was a very expensive camera with all the features to take professional quality pictures, but without focus, it was of little use. In this case, it became a source of frustration and disappointment. As far as my camera was concerned, I had never visited the United Sates.

I am afraid many of us go through life like I did on that trip—doing everything right, but being out of focus! We go through life and engage in many ideas but, in the end, nothing develops. To borrow from Erwin McManus' analogy, we are like kaleidoscopes in a world of telescopes and microscopes.[39] Kaleidoscopes are beautiful, and they

[39] McManus, Erwin Raphael, Wide Awake: The Future is Waiting Within You (Thomas Nelson, Nashville 2008), p. 123

mesmerize and inspire wonder in us. However, they lack clarity and depth of perception. Eventually, we need a telescope to have both the long view, and the microscope so we do not miss the critical details in life. In order to create the life you desire, sooner or later, you will need to begin to focus so you can see your life goals in 3-D as well as HD. You cannot love everywhere you go and everyone you meet. At some point, you will need to make a declaration of intent and live with purpose.[40]

You begin this process by narrowing your dream to a focal point. You take an inventory of your life—your preparation, your formal education, your life experiences, your likes and dislikes, your talents and gifts, your unique circumstances and your passion. Then you invite God to expand the boundaries of your imagination. You begin to see what God sees in you and the future He has planned that you may not even be aware of. As you reflect on these realities, a picture begins to emerge; one that allows you to know your assignment. You understand that God has been uniquely forming a "life-assignment" within you. Once you know your assignment, your existence becomes a liv-

[40] McManus, Erwin Raphael, Wide Awake: The Future is Waiting Within You (Thomas Nelson, Nashville 2008), p. 123

ing message to others. The things that have made up your life: your victories, your nagging problems, and those achievements that made you proud, those things that greatly humbled (and sometimes humiliated) you, those things that made you weak and the ones that brought joy—all conspire to tell God's story of redemption.

> *Your life is waiting for a passionate "yes" to bring focus and purpose. Without identifying what our big "yes" is, we will fall victim to having so much to do, so much to accomplish, with little time or resources to succeed.*

In 1992, I took a trip back to Kenya with two American friends and a friend from Brazil. The mission trip was a bit unfocused. We had fourteen days to get to about the same number of cities, towns, and villages scattered across what used to be the Eastern and Coast Provinces. About half of the trip was spent on the road, which should come as no surprise. Compulsive would be the word to describe our national trek, spending no more than two hours in some of the towns and villages. I do not know what meaningful ministry you can do in a community in two hours, unless you are walking through like Jonah, blasting fire and brimstone messages. To say the least, it was a false messianic complex (thinking we could save Kenya in 14 days) colliding with obsessive-compulsive disorder and a touch of attention deficit disorder! Looking back, this was not only one of the most costly mission trips I have ever taken, but also one that I cannot point to any lasting results from it. On one stretch of the trip, we went for five straight days without the convenience of taking a shower! We were suffering for Christ, so this was a small price to pay, so we thought. We were modern day David Livingstone or Johan Ludwig Krapf. Sadly, our unfocused activity produced only high costs, much tiredness with no lasting results. Not to mention, bewildered communities were left wondering, who were those strangers who came, set up PA system in the market place, hurriedly screamed sermons that did not connect, and left as quickly as they appeared?

My worst decisions often are those that I had to make quickly. The ones I had to decide now- with no time to think through.

Even the well intentioned can fall victim to too much "yes" and not enough "no." With so many distractions in today's world, it is easy to become less and less focused on the important things. Any one of us has the ability to make absolutely anything happen so long as we set a path and a daily action plan of execution in order to reach our ultimate goals.

Your life is waiting for a passionate "yes" to bring focus and purpose. Without identifying what our big "yes" is, we will fall victim to having so much to do, so much to accomplish, with little time or resources to succeed. When this happens, we end up falling into the category of mere dreamers. This is a polite way of saying that we become "idealists" who end up never accomplishing anything of eternal significance. You diminish your impact and dilute your contribution in life because you care about everything. You allow your passions to dissolve and diffuse when what you really need is focus.

Eventually, you end up self-medicating with apathy to keep your sanity. You may end up being cynical toward those who are passionate about life. When someone else's light shines too brightly, you complain about their passion. You respond with sarcasm—it doesn't take all that! However, when you are able to narrow down your passions and pursuits in order to find your life's true purpose, you can determine with absolute certainty where to focus your energy and embark on what Rick Warren described as "purpose driven life."[41]

If you ever lived out in the country where you had no electricity and had to use a spotlight in pitch darkness, you know what I mean by focus. When the spotlight (we called it "touch" back in the day) is not focused, the light gets diffused and you can hardly see the footpath or objects right in front of you. When you adjust the focus on the lens, you can see clearly. Similarly, you can choose to live with diffused light or you can develop the power of a focused life. McManus was correct when he wrote:

> *Focus allows you to live a life full of intensity, with all your passion fuelling your momentum in a singular direction. Focus isn't about less, but more. It is the ability to interconnect all you are and all you do around a central life theme. It is the difference between being a diffused light or a laser.*[42]

[41] Rick Warren's book, "The Purpose Driven Life," became a world sensation because it helped people find direction.

[42] Ibid, p. 125

The main reason that people struggle professionally and personally is simply due to a lack of focus. This lack of focus can be costly. It makes building a business difficult, developing a career impossible, and can throw major obstacles on your path to success. Being focused means that now you have the ability to ignore those distractions that tempt you away from your path.[43] It means that you have put time and thought into yourself and you know that each step you take is in the right direction.

Scatterbrain

Some people are blessed by being naturally focused. For the rest of us, maintaining focus presents a real and ever present challenge. This is how it is with me. Focus is counterintuitive to me. Early in my life, I wanted to be the Renaissance man; I wanted to know a little bit of everything. And if you went to school in Kenya like me, you know we were raised to be the proverbial jack-of-all-trades. Our education system wants to make sure we are well-rounded. The problem is that you cannot know everything, so you learn a little bit about a lot of things.

---

[43] Two years ago, I attended a meeting with Mike Murdock. This was perhaps the most important meeting I have attended. For the first time, I started understanding my assignment

In my case, I took math, science, languages, literature, history, geography, biology—you name it. I wanted to be the very best in everything. I was driven to be the best in class and in athletics; I was into soccer, track and field, and even tried basketball and volleyball, but standing at 5 feet 7 inches and with a vertical jump of only 4 inches, I could not make the teams.

You can choose to live with diffused light, or you can develop the power of a focused life. You belong to your choice

Of course, we all should know a little bit about math. In the words of my high school teacher, Mr. Mwanzia, only a fool can think life is possible without some knowledge of mathematics. You need to know if you are given correct change and keep up with your medications—two tablets three times a day—that sort of thing. Honestly, some people are just good at math, but the rest of us were there because some teachers thought that their assignment from God was to torment young students. Seriously, how many of us really need calculus? Is your job today dependent on your knowledge of the Pythagorean Theorem or your mastery of Euclidean geometry? I doubt it.

True, it is good to know that the Indian Ocean is not off the cost of Miami. It is good to know that one cannot drive from Kenya to the United States. As strange as it may seem, someone in Memphis, Tennessee, asked me how long it took me to drive to Kenya to the United States! Truth be told, few of us need expertise in geography or chemistry or biology. Like me, many are suffering from the Renaissance man syndrome—the jack-of-all-trades and master of none. Even if you did find your passion early in life, chances are, unless you have unusually understanding parents, they tried everything possible to convince you not to limit your options. No wonder in college we have a major and a minor—just in case.

You have to let even good dreams die when they are not supposed to be yours.

Then you go to college and change majors three or four times, which is about when your academic advisor comes up with a brilliant idea. There is this new major, you are told, general studies degree! It means you were all over the map and you never came down to any one thing. You were a generalist. While being a "generalist" is part of growing up, too many adults are still in that same regimen, and still carry with them that lack the focus that drives them away from the path uniquely cut out for them.

Let Good Dreams Die

If you are going to experience your life as it was meant to be lived, you have to learn to say no to all those other good options. The tough choices in life are not between the right and wrong options, but between all the seemingly good options that are simply not right for you. You have to let even good dreams die when they are not supposed to be yours.

The word "decide" is pregnant with meaning. In Latin, it expresses the idea "to cut." In that sense, every one of us is a surgeon. We go through life cutting away every potential future we reject and nurturing the one we choose. Every choice we make in favor of one option is also a choice against more possibilities that were competing for our time.

Similarly, the word focus comes from a Latin word that means *"hearth"* or *"fireplace."* In other words, it means the burning center.

The brighter and hotter your burning center, the more focused you will be in your life. The better you understand who God created you to be—complete with your unique gifts, passions talents, intelligence, all the gifts God has poured into you—the more you will begin to understand your unique place in human history.

> *The power of focus brings not only the strength of concentration but also the power of convergence.*

In order to function at peak performance, you must develop the competency of focus; you need to identify and lock into "your big yes" and embrace your mission in life. Focus gives you the capability to say no to all those other great and wonderful opportunities. You gain the courage to say no to those destructive choices that will derail your future. The power of focus brings not only the strength of concentration, but also the power of convergence. It helps you to harness all your talents, gifts, skills, passions, intellect, and experience—the whole of you—and brings it all together to unleash your highest potential. Without focus, not only do challenges overwhelm us, but we also become easily distracted and diffused by good opportunities. We suffer from the paralysis of choice. However, in order to make good choices, we must ask the right questions.

Cross-Examination

Have you ever noticed the critical role questions play in life? Court cases are won or lost on the strength of questions raised in cross-examination. When the defense attorney says, “I rest my case,” he implies that he has asked the question that nailed the witness. Have you rested your case in your life? Strategic planners often say that asking the right questions is about 80% of the key to find the right strategy. Great teachers effectively use the *“Socratic Method”* to ask penetrating questions to help students discover truth on their own.

Just take a moment and reflect on the powerful impact of questions on life. The trajectory of a life can be altered by simple but penetrating questions like:

- ***Will you marry me?***
- ***Have you decided on the job offer?***
- ***How do you feel about being a mother?***
- ***What kind of life can I expect after getting this diagnosis?***

When I preach, I usually interweave questions into my presentation. My goal is not to dump a lot of cognitive knowledge on my listeners, but to become a catalyst for the listeners to think, evaluate, and get to the core issues of their lives. God does not work at crossroads with His creation. You have to decide to focus and lock in on the direction God has called and prepared for you to live your life.

The Power of Concentration

The first step in getting focused is concentration. Concentration is directing all your energies and resources to a specific task, idea, and direction. Your potential becomes reality only when it is harnessed, developed, and deployed. Your talents become strengths when they are focused and directed. This is where you begin to discover who you are and the potential God has placed within you. Without a sense of destiny, you will diffuse your energy. However, when you are focused, you are the most powerful. "A destiny," wrote McManus, "is not something waiting for you, but something waiting within you."[44]

What Are You Looking At?

At an early age, I came upon this simple quote, "We become more

[44] McManus, p. 136

and more like that at which we constantly look."[45] The focus of your life should not be on your shortcomings, failures, weaknesses, guilt, shame or sin. Religion has done enough damage by thundering condemnations and focusing way too much on sin, guilt and shame.

Your talents become strengths when they are focused and directed.

I grew up in a shame-based culture where, if you wanted someone to shape up, the weapon of choice was to tell him or her: "Shame on you." Yes, you need to be aware of sin. You need to come clean and try not to cover it up transgressions. Yes, sin can cost you your dreams. Sin will take you further than you wanted to go, keep you longer than you wanted to stay, and cost you more than you are able to pay.

What you have at the core of your being shapes everything about the life you will live. As such, sin, guilt, and shame cannot be where God wants your focus to be. He wants us to focus on the unique nature of our creation—that we are created in His image and in His likeness.

[45] Increasingly, I have come to believe that outlook determines outcome. You attitude determines your altitude!

He wants us to focus on the truth: that we are designed to live a life beyond our wildest imaginations.

When we have this as our burning focus, as our burning center, we also develop the uncanny ability to see what others are missing. When others see the world as Chinua Achebe's world (things falling apart), you see things coming together. You see circumstances and people conspiring, not against you, but coming together for your good. You see all of us—humanity, all history, and all creation—as interconnected.

Everything that happens in life is interconnected, and your ability to focus brings it all together into one single story. You begin to understand that even pain can be redemptive. As such, you do not waste your pain by throwing a pity party. You know that if you throw a pity party, you will only have a company of one—you!

It should come as no surprise that the word "universe" means "one story." You see beyond the moment and into the future. You see beauty where others see decay. You see hope where others see despair. You see possibilities where others see impossibilities. You see God in everything. You see eternity when others only see history! You are a seer.

Scripture is filled with examples of focusing our lives, as well as what might happen if we lose our focus. One such example is recorded in Matthew 14: 22-31:

> *Immediately Jesus told his followers to get into the boat and go ahead of Him across the lake. He stayed there to send the people home. After he had sent them away, he went by himself up into the hills to pray. It was late, and Jesus was there alone. By this time, the boat was already far away from land. It was being hit by waves, because the wind was blowing against it. Between three and six o'clock in the morning, Jesus came to them, walking on the water. When his followers saw him walking on the water, they were afraid. They said, "It's a ghost!" and cried out in fear.*
>
> *But Jesus quickly spoke to them, "Have courage! It is I. Do not be afraid."*
>
> *Peter said, "Lord, if it is really you, then command me to come to you on the water." Jesus said, "Come." And Peter left the boat and walked on the water to Jesus. But when Peter saw the wind and the waves, he became afraid and began to sink. He shouted, "Lord, save me!" Immediately Jesus reached out his hand and caught Peter. Jesus said,*

"Your faith is small. Why did you doubt?"

(The Everyday Bible: New Century Version)

The Apostle Peter gets criticized a lot for being impetuous. So he is again, jumping into the water, taking several steps but then taking his eyes off Jesus and sinking. However, before you criticize him, have you ever walked on water? As far as we know, there are only two people who ever walked on water, Jesus and Peter. So Peter belongs to a very elite group of two. He obeyed a simple command, "come," and stepped out of the boat and started walking on water. This is the ultimate test of faith, to move on Jesus' word alone.

Focus allows you to live a life full of intensity with all your passions propelling your momentum in a singular direction.

We might ask, "Peter, how did you do it? Had you practiced, had you studied yoga, had you studied surface tension, or had you practiced levitation?"

Peter might have answered, "It was when I thought of surface tension, and yoga, and levitation, that I began to sink!" Faith rivets its attention solely on the Master who says, "Come."

Peter's experience exposes a dilemma we all face. Our surroundings and circumstances easily distract us, and all that is happening around us pulls our attention away from where we ought to be going.

Have you ever said to yourself, "If I could only see God and hear His voice audibly giving me blow-by-blow instructions, I would never lose my faith in Him." That is not true, however, because, like Peter, even with God right in front of us, telling us what to do ("come"), we lose focus and sink into despair. The answer is not for God to tell us exactly what to do for every single instance of our lives. Instead, the solution is to focus on what He has already directed you to do in His word, through revelation or by some other confirmed means. No matter how the inspiration comes to you, your job is to just do it (i.e. move forward, get up, etc.) without second-guessing and focusing on distractions.

Have you ever been in a meeting where you recommitted your life to Christ? You told God, I'm all in. I'm all yours. I'm fully committed.

However, later that afternoon, you are back to the habits you vowed you'd stop. The reason is simple, the distractions are right in your face—the job, the bills, the irritating spouse, the screaming kids and all. Peter could see and hear Jesus, but it didn't help. He still lost sight of his goal and allowed his circumstances to pull him off course.

As a side note, translators did not do a very good job in rendering this account. The translators were trying to help us when they translated, "Peter looked around, saw the waves and was terrified and begun to sink." However, in the original language, it says, "Peter saw the wind." The translators perhaps reasoned that no one would believe that Peter saw the wind, so they went with the effects of the wind—the waves.

As noted earlier, Peter could see and hear Christ, but this did not seem to help. To add to the irony, what caused him to lose sight was something invisible; he saw the wind. When he took his eyes from Jesus, his potential was diminished, and he began drowning in his own inadequacy.

Part of what robs us of the life we were created to live is that we don't lock in. We lose focus because we allow distractions to become bigger than our vision of God. We get knocked off our path because we start looking in the wrong direction, at the wrong things or people.

CHAPTER 12

Living Past the Edge

I am not naïve enough to think that this is the first book you've read on starting over or reaching for your life's dream. You have read stacks of books, scores of articles, and listened to countless motivational speeches about setting and achieving your goals. After all, we all begin with big dreams. Whey then do some of us achieve our dreams and advance in the face of adversity while others watch timidly from a distance and hope for a break that never seems to come?

In the first place, there is no such thing as easy breaks in life. There is no such thing as free lunch, and if you are waiting for something to turn up, you may as well start by rolling up your sleeves! Even if, by some miracle, someone gave you free lunch, you still would have to chew on it. In other words, you have to move your muscles. You have to work hard.

The fact is that the pursuit of having and doing it all has left many of us disappointed, discouraged, exhausted, defeated, anxious, stressed, and unable to enjoy any of what we have. Despite our sometimes superhuman exploits, we begin to build edges around our lives or rather accept that we have gone as far as we can go. In our disillusionment, we begin to think there is no possible way we can manage balancing a healthy marriage, great kids, fulfilling sex life, nurturing friends, and pursing God's given purpose.

What if the life you really want and the future God wants for you are hiding right now in your biggest problem, your worst failure, and your greatest fear?

When I lived in Nairobi, I helped a friend get what would have been his dream job. However, after a month or so, he called to tell me that he got fired. When I reached out to his boss to find out why my friend had lost his job, the boss told me that my friend always showed up late, left early, and while he was on the clock, he was stealing from the company.

"I have never known my friend to be a thief," I shot back in disbelief.

"Well, while at work, he was never productive," the boss explained. "He is a good man, but we don't pay people because they are good. We pay because they are productive." Later, I found out that my friend had allowed some invisible bullies in his life to stop his forward progress.

In other words, his life was organized for failure. It did not matter what opportunities were presented to him, sooner than later, he was going to run in to border bullies who would block him from advancing. He had never learned to live past the edge.

So why do some people seem to have the capacity to rebound from failure while the dreams of so many more seem helplessly out of reach? Bruce Wilkinson, author of The Prayer of Jabez and founder of Walk Thru the Bible, believes there is a direct relationship between realizing your dreams and battling fierce giants, or what he calls "border bullies." He identified four bullies that we must do battle with in order to reach our desired dream.

- **The Alarmist** ***says, "It's not safe." This bully is motivated by fear and tends to exaggerate the risks. This bully will be happy to see you spend the rest of your life in the land of familiar (your comfort zone).***

- **The Traditionalist** ***says, "That is not the way we do it." This bully does not like change. He or she often romanticizes the past (good old days) and is motivated by custom and routine. Imagine what***

would have happened if all the innovators had listened and re-coiled under the threats of this bully!

- **The Defeatist** ***says, "It's not possible." This bully (sometimes posing as your friend) sees problems everywhere and is certain that your big dreams won't and can't happen.***

- **The Antagonist** ***says, "I won't let you." This bully uses authority or intimidation to block your path. Antagonists may come against you because they fear they will lose money or control over your life or they may be just plain envious.***[46]

Who or what would you identify as a border bully in your life? For some, it may be a husband, wife, mother, father, or a close relative. To others, it may be past failures and disappointments. Whoever or whatever they are, why is this person or thing so significant as to prevent you from living the life God intended you to have? Is it possible that you are wasting energy focusing on the wrong thing?

---

[46] Wilkinson, Bruce4. The Dream Giver (Multnomah Publishers: Sisters, Oregon 2003), p.104.

If you reflect carefully, you will find that you have a friend or two who can help you in your journey. What people would you identify as buddies in your life? Who is it in your life that will go in the foxhole with you even when you are taking fire from all sides and you don't know if you will survive the enemy's onslaught? Look for friends who look on the bright side. Those who are willing to stand by you or at least remain neutral when you come under fire! Those who won't finish you off when you are wounded!

If you have one or two trues friends, they are a rare treasure. They are your dream champions. Often, these people enter our lives for a short period —a teacher or professor, for example. It could also be a boss or simply an opportunity of a lifetime. In my case, Dr. Wayne Allen was one of my dream champions. He was senior pastor at Briarwood Baptist Church, and I was his associate. I had barely begun the dissertation phase in my PhD study when tragedy struck and struck viciously. Our son was diagnosed with diabetes. A little earlier, my father had come down with stroke, which would keep him bedridden for two and half years.

The weight of having to provide for my growing family, financially care for my father in Kenya, take my son to endless doctor's appointments while providing emotional support as he dealt with this devastating illness (he was the first and only known diabetic on both sides of the family), handle my masters' level student teaching load, write my dissertation, and carry out full ministerial load at the church was overwhelming. I went to Dr. Wayne and told him that I was dropping out of the PhD program. I did not see how I could manage to balance all these responsibilities. However, he would have none of that. He saw in me what I couldn't as a young PhD student. "Not under my watch," he said. "Chances are, if you drop out of the program, you will never come back to complete your degree."

How did Dr. Wayne champion my dream? He quietly rearranged my responsibilities so I could spend more time in the office researching and writing. He told me, "Robert, some of the other staff members may be jealous about this arrangement, but I want you to have this. I want you to stay here for a long time, but I believe God has a bigger and brighter future for you than this church."

Wayne helped me to overcome my border bully—the alarmist standing in the way of completing my PhD work with the words, "It cannot happen." I had every excuse to drop out of the program—a sick child, an ailing father, ministry responsibilities at the church, family responsibilities, and so on. I had proof that it could not be done. Other students I considered more gifted than I had dropped out of the program. Eight students had been accepted into the program, but by the time I was considering bailing out, we were down to two! I had allowed myself to be drawn into collective reasoning. I had accepted conventional wisdom that, when faced with insurmountable obstacles, you look for the exit sign.

There is no such thing as collective brain. There is no such thing as collective thought. You must think and shape your own thoughts

However, as it were, the mind is an attribute of an individual. There is no such thing as a collective brain. There is no such thing as collective thought. Even an agreement reached by a group of people is only a compromise or an average drawn from an aggregate of individual thoughts. It is a secondary consequence, a byproduct, so to speak. The primary act—the process of reasoning—must be undertaken by each man alone. We can divide a meal among ourselves, but we cannot digest it in a collective stomach. No man can use his lungs to breath for another. All the functions of body and spirit are private. They cannot be shared or transferred.

Sure, we inherit the products of the thoughts of others. We inherited the wheel; then we made an automobile. The moving force that propels us past the edge is the creative faculty that takes the inherited idea as raw material and uses it to originate the next step. As such, all learning is the exchange of material. No man can give the other the capacity to think past the accepted limits; no man can propel you past the edge. Nothing is given to man; everything he needs must be produced. Every discovery brings us on the edge, where we are confronted by two alternatives. We survive in only one of two ways: by the independent work of our own mind or as a parasite fed by the minds of others.

The creator, the one, who dares to go past the edge, originates. The parasite borrows. The creator faces odds alone. The parasite faces odds through an intermediary.

The creator, the one, who dares to go past the edge, originates. The parasite borrows. The creator faces odds alone. The parasite faces odds through an intermediary. I grew up in a culture that promoted "parasite thinking." To get a job, you needed a "big man" in high office to push you through. However, even as a young man, I revolted against this *"parasite thinking."* I was determined to blaze a new trail. I was not going to cut corners. I was not going to slither. I coined a personal motto: *I would rather fail temporarily with the truth and ultimately succeed than succeed temporarily with falsehood and ultimately fail.*

The creator's concern is the conquest of nature. The parasite's concern is the conquest of men. The basic need of a second-hander—a parasite—is to secure his ties with people in order to be sustained. He places relationships first, but only so he can enlarge his pool of social capital from which to draw his livelihood.

We have the false belief that the highest virtue is to give. While this is true, it cannot be first. We cannot give what we do not have. *Creation comes before distribution; or else, pretty soon, there would be nothing to distribute.* The need for the creator—the originator, the one striving to go past the edge—comes before the need of the beneficiary.

When we take a flight, for example, we are told before takeoff that, in the unlikely event that we run out of oxygen, masks will drop from the ceiling. When this happens, reach for the mask, securely place it over your nose so you can breathe normally, and then help your dependents travelling with you. At first, I thought that was the most selfish thing I had ever heard. If I am traveling with my child or my elderly parent, shouldn't I help them first? It may seem counterintuitive, but it is the only sure way to make certain that both you and your dependents survive.

To move on with God, you have to be willing to break ranks with mediocrity and bravely push your way past the border bullies that have been holding you back. You must become that rugged individual—the creator, the originator—who, even though denied, oppressed, persecuted, and exploited, does not give excuses but rather moves forward, carrying all humanity along with him by the power given by God.

CHAPTER 13

Beating the Odds

Neal Rose, in his book *If Only*, made an insightful distinction between two kinds of regrets: *regrets of action* and *regrets of inaction*. Regrets of action occur when you wish you had not done something like make a commitment to start a relationship. In theological terms, we call these sins of commission. To the contrary, a regret of inaction is wishing you had done something. In theological terms, we call these sins of omission.

> *Think of it as a farmer whose preoccupation is a clean garden and spends his time pulling weeds. At the end of the season, he may end up with a very clean garden, but no harvest.*

As mentioned earlier in this book, I am convinced that the church has fixated on sins of commission for far too long. We have a long list of do's and don'ts. To put it in another way, we think we can achieve holiness by subtraction. Right living, we think, is a byproduct of subtracting something from our lives that shouldn't be there. Think of it as a farmer whose preoccupation is a clean garden and spends his time pulling weeds. At the end of the season, he may end up with a very clean field, but will have no harvest. I think God is concerned about sins of omission—those things we should have done and could have done. Goodness is not the absence of badness. You can do nothing wrong and still do nothing right. Those who simply run away from sin are like half-baked cakes or, in this case, half-Christians, if there is such thing as a half-Christian. Our calling is far higher than just running away from sins. Our calling is about participating in God's extraordinary life. In the words of the prophet: "those who know their God shall grow strong and do exploits."

When Righteous Isn't Enough

The most concentrated example of the teachings of Jesus is found in Matthew 5-7, a passage often referred to as the Sermon on the Mount but which, in other ways, is Jesus' Kingdom Manifesto. If we want to understand the essential elements of Jesus' central message, there is no better place to look than here. In sections of this message, Jesus goes hard after religious leaders of his day whose focus was merely on external conformity to the law and technical outward perfection. He points out that outward righteousness is not righteous enough and inserts this odd exhortation:

> *"You have heard that it was said, 'You must not be guilty of*

adultery.' But I tell you that if anyone looks at a woman and wants to sin sexually with her, in his mind he has already done that sin with the woman. If your right eye causes you to sin, take it out and throw it away. It is better to lose one part of your body than to have your whole body thrown into hell. If your right hand causes you to sin, cut it off and throw it away. It is better to lose one part of your body than for your whole body to go into hell."

(Matthew 5:27-30 NCV)

Jesus used grotesque imagery of physical self-mutilation to convey the horror of self-inflicted spiritual mutilation by lust. He pointed to the inward fragmentation endured by those insisting on outward moral and ethical conformity without purity of the heart. Philosopher Dallas Willard succinctly pointed out:

"If not doing anything wrong is the goal, then that could be achieved by dismembering yourself and making actions impossible. What you cannot do, you certainly will not do. Remove your eye, your hand, etc., therefore and you will roll into heaven a mutilated stump. The price of dismemberment

would be small compared to the reward of heaven. That is the logical conclusion for one who held the beliefs of the Scribes and the Pharisees...He reduces their principle—that righteousness lies in not doing anything wrong—to the absurd, in the hope that they will forsake their principle and see and enter the righteousness that is beyond the righteousness of the Scribes and the Pharisees—beyond, where compassion and love, not sacrifice, is the fundamental thing."[47]

The more risks you take the easier taking risks become. Seizing the raw and unshaped opportunities becomes second nature.

Is anyone else tired of reactive Christianity that is known more for what it's against than what it is for? When Jesus addresses issues of sexuality, for instance, He makes it clear that the kingdom of God is not a matter of the pelvis, but rather a matter of the heart. Conventional morality defines purity by avoidance, Jesus provides a radically different set of value system with the words, "Blessed are the pure in heart."

[47] Willard, Dallas, "Jesus the Logician," Christian Scholar's Review 28, no. 4 (1999), 605-14, available at www.dwillard.org

This calls for going against the grain—swimming upstream, so to speak. Any dead fish can be carried along the currents and bounce along the waves. It takes a live fish to swim against the current. Faced with tough conditions, impossible is the word that comes to the minds of many. It is easier, much easier, to go with the flow. I have had many believers come to me with issues and, when I attempt to offer counsel, the words they utter are, "Pastor, you just don't know what I am up against." In order to reach your God-given potential and fulfill your God-given destiny, you have to do something counterintuitive. Some of your actions won't make sense this side of eternity, but those who blaze new trails know that God is connecting the dots in ways they can't comprehend. They don't make excuses when faced with insurmountable odds. They are out to beat the odds.

> ***Faith is embracing uncertainty and moving forward in spite of the circumstances.***

Odds Are Overrated

What is worse than being in a pit? It is being in a pit on a snowy day. What is worse than being in a pit on a snowy day? It is being in a pit in a snowy day with a lion. What is worse than being in a pit on a snowy day with a lion?

It is being in a pit on a snowy day with a lion and having a 9-foot giant wielding a 14-foot spear waiting for you when and if you get out of the pit. Now that is what you call being in the pits!

In the book of 1 Chronicles 11, we find the conclusion of the special record of the unusually brilliant and sensational achievements of the mighty men of King David. Here, we find one of the most inspiring passages of scripture:

> *"Benaiah son of Jehoiada was a brave fighter from Kabzeel who did mighty things. He killed two of the best warriors from Moab. He also went down into a pit and killed a lion on a snowy day. Benaiah killed an Egyptian who was about eight and one-half feet tall and had a spear as a weapon. Benaiah had a club, but he grabbed the spear from the Egyptian's hand and killed him with his own spear. David made him leader of his bodyguards. These were the things Benaiah son of Jehoiada did. He was as famous as the three.*

He received more honor than the thirty, but he did not become a member of the three. David made him leader of his bodyguards."

(1 Chronicles 11:22-25)

Did you get that? Benaiah slayed two of Moabites mightiest men, took down a huge Egyptian, and killed a lion in a pit on a snowy day! Just so you know, this is not a fable. It is not poetic license. It is not hyperbole. This is recorded history. It is factual. The same encounter is repeated in 2 Samuel 23: 20-23.

Let me state the obvious here. Benaiah was outnumbered and overmatched in all these encounters. The odds were not in his favor in any of these situations, yet he still succeeded.

Improbable Odds

I am not a betting man, but if I'm placing my bet on an average size Israelite armed with a club or a giant Egyptian with a spear, I'm going to put my money on guy standing at almost 9 feet tall with the sharp pointed weapon. However, the superior weapon advantage is only a part of the battle narrative. According to Scripture, the Egyptian stood at 8 ½ feet tall. Add shoes to that and a helmet, and the man gets to be about 9 feet tall.

In the world of boxing, the tale of the tape is a major consideration in guessing who is favored to win the bout. A fighter with a longer reach has a decisive advantage over a shorter boxer. So given his height, I would guess the Egyptian giant had a 20- to 25-inch reach advantage. Add the 14-foot weapon advantage and the size advantage together, and you have a mismatch the likes of David and Goliath. He is much taller, much heavier, and has a better weapon. This is a no brainer. However, as the story unfolds, I would have lost my money. The man with the club wins. And he does it by wrestling the spear from the Egyptian giant and slaying him with his own spear. Personally, I want to see the instant replay of Benaiah wrestling the spear from the Egyptian. How did he even sneak up on him to get close enough to grab it?

I don't even know how you begin to calculate the odds of man going mano-o- mano against a lion in a pit on a snowy day. In Benaiah's case, it was a hand to claw combat fought out in an area where his movement was highly restricted. Not only do fully-grown lions weigh up to 500 pounds and run 35 mph, but their vision is also five times better than a human with 20/20 vision. This lion had a huge advantage in a dimly lit pit. And I guarantee that a sure-footed lion with cat-like agility certainly gains the upper paw in snowy, dark, dump, and slippery conditions.

God is in the business of strategically positioning us in the right place at the right time, but there are times when the right place seems like the wrong place and the right time feels like the wrong time

Scripture doesn't tell us what Benaiah was doing or where he was going when he encountered this lion. Chances are, he was not looking for trouble. He was going about his life, minding his own business. Then, as he was walking along, he caught the sight of a lion from the corner of his eye.

Sometimes we choose our battles and, at other times, battles are thrust on us by a strange twist of circumstances. Some of the battles we fight should never have been fought; someone should have just walked away. Maturity demands that we know when to give chase and when to call off the pursuit, knowing when to repair a broken relationship and when to replace it. Losses are compounded when we hold on to people we should have released or let people go we should have kept.

The way of wisdom is to know the things we need to stay clear of, things that can easily and needlessly sap our strength and resources. There are negative areas that it would be unwise for me to stray into. There are foolish arguments I must avoid and needless fights I must stay out of because there are other times and places where I will need my strength.

Benaiah did not choose this battle. It chose him, and his reaction was daring. Usually when the sight of a man-eating beast enters a person's vision, the image travels through the optic nerve and registers in the visual cortex, where the brain has one overarching message: *run away as fast as you can.* Normal people run away from lions. They are controlled by the reflex reaction of self-preservation. However, lion chasers are wired differently.[48] They run toward their lions.

Choose Your Battles Wisely

"You cannot die on every hill," I remember a popular preacher telling

---

[48] Batterson, Mark. In A Pit With a Lion on a Snowy Day: How to Survive And Thrive When Opportunity Roars (Multnomah Books: NY, 2006) p. 16.

us in chapel in my senior year in seminary. Maturity demands that you learn to pick your battles wisely. When I was young, I used to get into very foolish fights. On the schoolyard, there was a bully who would dare me to cross a line or to level some dirt he had heaped on the ground. In my youthful stupidity, my response was, "Oh, yeah?" I would cross the line or kick up the pile of dirt, and with that, a fight would start that, at times, would spill over to involve boys from the entire village. In addition, the final outcome would not be decided until the last day of school. Those were foolish battles.

> *"A low view of God is the cause of a hundred lesser evils." But a person with a "high view" of God "is relieved of ten thousand temporal problems."*
>
> *-A. W. Tozer*

Doesn't it seem like Benaiah is choosing his battles poorly? He is out-manned and out-sized, but this guy goes on to become Commander-in-Chief of Israel's army. If you're Commander-in-Chief, you better know how to choose your battles wisely!

On one level, this seems like a mistake, but what if Benaiah had defeated a single Moabite who looked like Peewee Herman or Tom Thumb? Or what if Benaiah had defeated an Egyptian dwarf? Or suppose he chased a scary cat into a pit on a sunny day, pulled it out by the tail, and smashed it against a tree? I'm pretty sure we wouldn't be reading about it. Why? It's not a big deal if the odds were in his favor.

I am not sure that too many of us like being in pits with lions on snowy days, but those are the stories worth telling. Overcoming these type of experiences make life worth living. Lion chasers don't try to avoid situations where the odds are against them. Lion chasers know that impossible odds set the stage for amazing miracles.

Here's the rest of the story. Finding yourself in a pit with a lion on a snowy day seems to qualify as really bad day. However, stop and think about it. When King David is looking for his personal security detail, guess whose resume he will zero in on? If the king needed a fearless man to protect him, he had just found his man in Benaiah, a man with a great resume and the scars to back it up.

He Is An On Time God

There is a pattern repeated in scripture and in real life: sometimes God does not intervene until something is humanly impossible. He comes in just in the nick of time. This truth is beautifully expressed in a song from the African American experience:

He's an on time God, Yes He is

Oh . . .an on time God, Yes He is

Job said

He may not come when you want Him

But He'll be there right on time

I'll tell ya He's an

On time God, yes He is

You can ask the children of Israel, trapped at the Red Sea, by that mean old Pharaoh and his army. They had water all around them, and Pharaoh on their track.

From out of nowhere, God stepped in and cut a highway, just like that.

Now let me tell you he's an . . .

You can ask the five thousand, hungry souls he fed, on the banks of the river, with two fish and five loaves of bread,

what a miracle, He performed for the multitude.

Oh what He did way back then He'll do today

for me and you. . .

This, I think, reveals a dimension of God's personality: He loves the impossible. I love that, and I get a kick out of doing things people didn't think I could do. As a child, I turned everything into a dare. Everything was a challenge. It didn't matter whether we were walking down a dirt road or sharing a meal, I would challenge: Do you think I can outrun you running backwards to that fence post? Do you think I can walk on my hands to that tree over there? Do you think I can eat 10 mangoes in one minute?

If someone said yes, I didn't even bother trying. What's the point of doing something my friends already knew I could do? I would raise the stakes until someone thought I couldn't do it. Then I would attempt the impossible as all my friends looked on to see me fail. Is there any greater accomplishment than doing what nobody thinks you can do?

Whether it is Benaiah or Gideon, whose army of 32,000 was reduced to 300, God comes to the aid of his people when the odds are stacked against them. In Gideon's case, it even gets more interesting. The odds had to be one in a million at this point; then God told Gideon to attack his enemies with trumpets and jars! What? If noise was the strategy, don't you think 32,000 raucous soldiers would make more noise than 300?

If noise was the strategy, don't you think 32,000 soldiers would make more noise than 300?

Israel triumphed and God got the glory. When an army of 300 routes the enemy with jars and trumpets as their only weapons and wins, then only God can get the glory. Their victory could not have been explained any other way apart from God's will and power.

Often, our prayers revolve around asking God to reduce the odds against us; we want everything to work in our favor. However, perhaps God wants to stack the odds against us so we can experience a miracle of a greater magnitude.

Contingency Plans

Second Kings 6th chapter records one of the most ridiculous prayers ever recorded. A group of prophets were chopping wood to build additional living quarters because the existing dormitory was too small. As they were hard at work, one of the prophet's ax heads flew lose and dropped in the river. The junior prophets cried out to Elisha, "Alas master! For it was borrowed." Is this a prayer? Is he asking for help, or is this the prophet's equivalent of the sort of words a construction worker would utter when he smashes his finger with a hammer while driving a nail?

Whatever the case, notice the tense. The junior prophet uses the past tense: it was borrowed. As far as he is concerned, this ax head is as good as gone. This expresses the sentiments in Jack Handley's Deep Thoughts:

If you drop your keys in a river of molten lava
Let 'em go, man, 'cause they're gone!

Like Handley's saying, this junior prophet regarded his loss as final. He had no expectation whatsoever of recovering it. I suppose he wanted a little sympathy and, at least, a contingency plan. Now that I have lost a borrowed ax head, what do I do next? I have no money to repay the owner and I don't even know how to face the owner since I had promised that I would take care of his only ax head. And just like that, it's gone. The very thing I feared most has happened to me. Now what?

At least, unlike most of us, he acknowledged his loss. How many of us have lost our cutting edge? How many of us have had our lives dulled by circumstances? However, rather than acknowledging our loss, we keep whacking at life, we keep chopping wood with the shaft, when we know all too well that we lost our ax head. Meanwhile, we over-compensate by making harder blows.

Although this junior prophet acknowledged his loss immediately, he couldn't have guessed what would happen next, and for good reason. Any object with a density greater than 1 gram per cubic centimeter does not float on water. Cast iron has a density of approximately 7.2 grams per cubic centimeter. This means that iron heads cannot float in water. Even fishhooks sink straight down the bottom of the lake.

Iron doesn't float on water or does it? There is only one way to find out. Pray a crazy prayer! However, before we bow our heads in prayer, the story gets even more ridiculous. First of all, if I was Elisha, I would have felt sorry for this guy who is obviously stressed about the loss. That said, my first reaction would be to offer him my ax head or drive him to the nearest Home Depot to buy a replacement. It would not even cross my mind to pray. If I dared to pray, I would offer one of those pious prayers. You know those prayers that sound pious but are filled with unbelief. It would sound like this:

> *Our Heavenly Father, the God of impossibilities, I know that ax heads have a density greater than 7.2 grams per cubic centimeter. I know that at body temperature, no liquid has a viscosity as low as water. However, with all these limitations, would you please consider overruling the laws of physics and doing what has never been done before? Please make this ax head swim or lead us to someone who can help us with a magnet to locate and retrieve it. If this is your will, do it for your honor and glory. Amen.*

Then after prayer, I would ask if anyone has information where we can get a magnet to try to sweep the bottom of the river. However, he didn't pray—not right away, anyway. Instead, Elisha asked the apprentice where the ax head fell. If I was the junior prophet, I would be wondering, “What difference does it make? The thing is in the bottom of this muddy water, sir!” Obediently, but perhaps reluctantly, he points to the place where the ax head fell in the water. Elisha cuts a stick and dips it at the spot, and something happened that had never happened before or has ever happened since.

God is great, not because nothing is too big for him.
He is great because nothing is too small for him either.

The ax head floated.

Now, as exciting as this miracle is, when you think about it, it's interesting for several reasons. First, it ranks very low in the order of tragedies; it is not exactly a life-or-death situation. Yes, it is a borrowed ax head, and true, it is lost. However, it's only an ax head! Either way you cut it, overdramatize it, or sensationalize it, it's still nothing more than an ax head.

It was like bringing a tooth pick to a gun battle

It may seem uncaring, but don't we need to save miracles for more tragic events? In the order of tragedies, it ranks right up there with the miracle at Cana of Galilee, where Jesus turned water into wine to save face for a young bride and groom because they had failed to stock up enough wine for their wedding reception. If we run out of wine, the worst thing we might face is a little embarrassment. People will grumble a little, drink Kool-Aid, go home, and forget it in a few days, right?

Secondly, and most importantly, the point about these minor miracles is: God cares about the little details of our lives. He cares about wedding receptions and lost ax heads as much as he cares about Lazarus' death. God is great, not because nothing is too big for him. He is great because nothing is too small for him either. He cares about the next step you are considering taking. He wants to go with you into your future. He is prepared to help you refocus your life. And he answers your ridiculous prayers.

To the infinite, all things are finite.

In our thinking, we have easy requests and difficult problems. We have big problems and small challenges. However, has it ever occurred to you that to the infinite, all things are finite? The ultimate value of these kinds of miracles is to help us redefine reality, and the reality is that nothing is too difficult for or insignificant to God. He is just as interested in the helping you with the seemingly ridiculous stuff as he is in helping you with the most life-threatening challenges you will ever face. He can help you with your $1,000 need as easily as he can with $10,000. The zeroes before the decimal do not scare Him one bit!

A common thread runs through all these biblical accounts: the elements of faith and obedience. Without faith, it is impossible to please God (Heb. 11:6). There are four components to true faith:

1. ***Reckons***
2. ***Risks***
3. ***Rests***
4. ***Receives***

True faith reckons; that is, it does not bury its head in the proverbial sand and deny that there is a problem. Benaiah knew he was chasing a lion, not a scary cat. The disciples knew they did not have enough resources to feed 5,000 hungry men, not counting women and children. They knew when they found a young boy with five loaves and two fish, they only had enough to feed no more than seven adults, and that was really stretching it. For all practical purposes, this was the young boy's lunch. The disciples crunched the numbers, but any way they sliced five loaves of bread and two fish, they still came up 4,993 meals short.

How do we get our faith strengthened? Not by striving after faith, but by resting on the Faithful One, Christ our Lord.

Elisha's servant knew he was in trouble with his neighbor the moment the ax head flew from the shaft in his hand and sunk in that river. Similarly, Lazarus' sisters knew that their brother was dead, not merely in a comma or taking a siesta.

Real faith risks all; it risks ridicule, looking foolish, and failure. Gideon's army was outnumbered and risked fighting with the unconventional tactic of beating on jars and blowing trumpets. It was like bringing a toothpick to a gun fight! However, *true faith also rests*. When you trust God, you can rest knowing that He will do what He says he will do. This kind of faith is beautifully expressed in the last stanza of the hymn, "Standing on the Promises."

Standing on the promises I cannot fall,
Listening every moment to the Spirit's call
Resting in my Savior as my all in all,
Standing on the promises of God.

Ultimately, *true faith receives* what is supposes. Matthew 21:22 says, *"You can pray for anything, and if you have faith, you will receive it."* (NLT) When we ask and trust God completely, we will receive what seems miraculous, improbable and unlikely to others outside the faith. This truth is rooted in the scripture, *". . . because everyone who is born from God has overcome the world. Our faith is the victory that overcomes the world."* (1 John 5:4 ISV)

Chapter 14

Putting It All Together

Let me recap a few ideas on how to put an end to passive observers, paralyzed by the need for a perfect opportunity, and start seizing the raw, unshaped potential for your life with God. I will have succeeded in reaching my objective of writing this book if I have helped you to learn to recognize your *"Divine Moment"* and grab hold of it with force.

To make the most of everything you have read in *"Make a Fresh Start with God,"* here are a few concluding thoughts that you need to keep in mind:

Overcome Misconceptions

> *Life is full one small step; one giant leap moments. These are seemingly small steps with the potential to alter the trajectory of your life forever*

Have you ever been most afraid of doing the very thing you were certain would spur your life to success? Have you had the problem of having to draw back from achieving the life of your dream again and again? Do you have a hard time understanding why you won't leave your comfort zone?

The closer we get to our breakthrough, the more anxious we get and the more likely we are to doubt our pending success. These misconceptions will keep us in our comfort zones if we allow them. Here are three very dangerous misconceptions:

Comfort Zone Misconception #1:

Because I feel fear, my idea must not be from God.

I can tell you from personal experience, biblical accounts, and historical proofs that this is just not true. Anyone who has ever attempted anything great had to deal with fear. In fact, the opposite is true; if you are not afraid, your dream is not from God. It is not big enough. God only gives God-sized dreams and makes God-sized assignments.

> *The price of your vitality is the sum of your fears.*
>
> *David Whyte*

Think back over the times you have attempted to take a big step into a new territory. When you failed, did you begin to doubt whether you were cut out for this? Did you think that perhaps this task was not meant for you?

This misconception leads to a second one:

Comfort Zone Misconception #2:

I can't go forward if God doesn't take away my fear.

In my experience, God rarely makes our fears disappear. Instead, He asks us to be strong and courageous in the face of our fears. "In war, there is no substitute for victory," said General Douglas MacArthur.[49] In any case, if there is a substitute, not too many of us would want the substitute: defeat or death.

Life is not a playground. Life is a battlefield. God isn't looking for volunteers because every one of us is a soldier.[50] Some are good soldiers,

[49] In his farewell speech to the American Congress, April 19, 1951, General Douglas MacArthur said these words: In war, there is no substitute for victory.

[50] The key to being victorious is learning how to put God's power to work in your life in spite of your fears.

and others are fighting the wrong wars. Still, there are others who are AWOL in the arena of life.

> *To be certain of God means we are uncertain of all our ways; we do not know what a day may bring forth. This is said generally with a sign of sadness; it should rather be an expression of breathless expectation*
>
> *Osward Chambers*

Comfort Zone Misconception #3

I cannot move forward until all my doubts are cleared.

One thing that God does with doubt is He uses it to "burn up" any bad spiritual fuel that we are using for our souls. We are forced to hang on when His plans do not make sense. We learn to live with unanswered questions. We come to see and accept that it is okay if we do not have all the answers.

Writer G.K. Chesterton once said that a madman is "someone who is in the clean and well-lit prison of one idea: he is sharpened to one painful point. He is without healthy hesitation and healthy complexity."[51]

[51] Chesterton, G.K., Orthodoxy (New York: Doubleday, 2001) pp. 16-17

Early in my ministry, I felt that my duty as a preacher was to defend God. I felt it was my responsibility to present an unwavering spiritual front, even if that meant not being completely honest about my misgivings. I felt people expected me to have all the answers. So I resorted to hiding my suspicions deep down inside and safely locking them away in a dark corner closet in the basement of my mind. This, I convinced myself, would inspire people. My certainty, albeit untrue, would somehow rub off on others and give them assurance as well. I could get away with it because, for years, I was an itinerant evangelist. After I accepted my first church as pastor in Union City Tennessee, everything changed. It was easy to impress people from a distance, but harder to impact people up close.

A few years of serving people in churches has now cured all that foolishness. Before, I had all the answers, but now, I'm not even sure I know which questions to ask. Helping the chronically unemployed, visiting four year olds with leukemia in children's hospitals, praying with women who have been violently raped, and counseling people with mental illness has a way of removing all those false pretenses.

I quickly embraced three words that I use often these days: "I don't know." I don't know why you lost your son or daughter. I don't know why God gave you the parents he did. I don't know why you did everything right, but your husband still left you for a man, much less another woman. I don't know why my parents died just months before I earned my PhD and got to the point where I could take care of them financially. I don't know why a lot of things happen anymore, and that's okay.

> *I have since learned to embrace uncertainty or rather the duality of nature. The imprecise measurement of initial conditions precludes the precise prediction of future outcomes. Thus, my doubts won't keep me from moving forward.*

One thing I know, though, is this: after the last grain of sand has been washed from under your feet, it is then that you will know after all that you were standing on a rock.

Cozy Can Be a Trap

Among other things, our comfort zone keeps us from starting over and reaching for our dreams even when we know that is what we are supposed to do. It is not easy to break out of our comfort zone; after all, we have spent much of our time building it. A comfort zone is our warm blanket of relationships. It is the insulation of predictable routines that make us feel safe and good. It is the security fence of acceptable behavior. It is the concrete pavement on the path of our past successes and failures.[52]

For Moses, it was a big fall from being the prince of Egypt to become an obscure shepherd in the backside of the nation. Moses was in his cozy comfort zone while he tended his father in-law's sheep. It wasn't what he wanted, but as a man wanted for murder, it was better than having to look over his shoulder. At least the sheep wouldn't tell on him.

Our comfort zone completely surrounds us with the familiar and makes us feel safe. Here, we know what's coming tomorrow and the day after that. Outside of that, who knows? I am not suggesting we live recklessly or thoughtlessly. Yet, we must agree that our big dream

[52] Wilkinson, The Dream Giver, p. 88

always lie outside our comfort zone. At some point, we are just going to have to break through our comfort zone and step into the realm of the unfamiliar and uncomfortable.

God Loves Ordinary People

God loves ordinary people, otherwise, He wouldn't have created so many of us. Often, many of us feel like we are permanently certified nobodies. We are unremarkable, invisible, and stuck! As John Maxwell observes, the difference between ordinary and extraordinary is the little word "extra."[53]

Somehow we all know that playing it safe
is a sure formula to lose the game.

One of my favorite nobodies was a lady by the name Agnes Bojaxhiu of Albania. She never had a college degree, never married, and never owned a car. However, she had a huge dream: to live out her faith by caring for "the lost, the last, and the least of these." She gave away her life to serve and care for the dying and poorest of the poor.

[53] Maxwell John C. Think on These Things: Meditations for Leaders (Beacon Hill Press, Kansas: KS 1990), p, 48

Today, we know her as Mother Teresa, Nobel Prize winner and one of the most admired people of our century. She spent most of her life caring for the poor and the dying in Calcutta, India. Even in her death, she continues to touch lives with God's love. Through her Sisters of Charity, her big dream is still changing millions of people around the world.

Whatever your situation today, you were made to be someone special. You are a limited edition of one. Don't wait another day. Allow God to ignite your God-sized dream and be open to His work of grace in your life.

Seize Your Divine Moment

If you could capture one moment in your life, which one would it be? Would it be a moment you took a risk on something that turned out to be a great blessing or a moment of regret? How many of us have spent many hours reflecting on lost opportunities without recognizing that those lost moments are just that—lost? We cannot reenact lost moments. We cannot recapture time.

If you could take one moment and squeeze every ounce of opportunity out of it, would that not be a moment in the future rather than in the past? What if you knew that somewhere in front of you is a moment that could change your life forever, a moment pregnant with potential, a moment filled with limitless possibilities? What if you knew there was a moment coming, a divine moment, one in which God would meet you in such a way that nothing would be the same again? What if it was such a defining moment in which the choice you made could change the trajectory and the momentum of your future?[54]

How would you react to that moment? How would you prepare for it? Would you even be able to identify it when it came? Moments are as numerous as the sand on the seashore and any of them could prove to be your most significant one. So, however mundane a moment may appear, the miraculous may well be waiting to be unwrapped within it.

Cape Diem is a Latin phrase popularized in a poem by Horace.[55] It is commonly translated "seize the day." Deriving from the Latin word

---

[54] We do not have the privilege of knowing upfront the significance of a moment. When a moment is missed, you get a glimpse of at an opportunity lost. When you imagine, you look to a moment still to come. The only moment you are responsible for is the one right in front of you. The Biblical imagery of a moment is the blink of an eye. In other words, do not blink, or your will miss it.

[55] Harrison, S. J. The Cambridge Companion to Horace (Cambridge Press, 2012) Pp. 154, 168

"carpo," it literally means "I pick, pluck, cull, crop, gather; I want." There may well be other moments waiting behind this one, this time, this year, but the moment you are in right now is waiting to be seized.

Just a Moment

A number of years ago, a friend at the North American Mission Board shared with me this poem by an unknown author:

I have only just a minute,
Only sixty seconds in it.
Forced upon me, can't refuse it.
Didn't seek it, didn't choose it.
But it's up to me to use it,
I must suffer if I lose it,
Give account if I abuse it.
Just a tiny little minute,
But eternity is in it.[56]

Though we cannot live life in a hurry, we can live with a sense of urgency. We can live with passion. This, I believe, is what the Apostle

[56] Moments move in a timely manner and time waits for no one.

Paul was speaking of when he wrote to the church at Ephesus, "Make the most of every opportunity in these evil days." (Ephesians 5:16 NLT) Henri Frederic Amiel wisely observed, *"Without passion, man is a mere latent force and possibility, like the flint which awaits the shock of the iron before it can give forth its spark."* Soren Kierkegaard warned, *"Most men pursue pleasure with such breathless haste that they hurry past it."*

> *Twenty years from now you will be more disappointed by the things you didn't do than by the ones you did do. So throw off the bowlines. Sail away from the safe harbor. Catch the trade winds in your sails.*
>
> *Explore. Dream. Discover*
>
> *Mark Twain*

McManus penned this helpful statement, *"One of the Greek words from which we get the English word moment is* ***atomos****. You can easily see the word* ***atom*** *and* ***atomic*** *come from atomos."*[57] This is a perfect

[57] McManus, Dare to Live a life of Adventure: Seizing your Divine Moment (Thomas Nelson, 2002), p. 11

picture of what is hidden behind a moment. And within the atomic, there is nuclear capacity in the rapid release of energy in the fission[58] of heavily atomic nuclei. When you seize your moment, you ignite an atomic reaction. You become a human catalyst creating a powerful impact on your life and the life of your loved ones. The journey begins right now, in this moment. Whatever you do, do not underestimate what your fresh start with God may hold.

Un-learn Your Fears

In this book, I have touched on crucial areas of life that I consider critical to making a fresh start with God. The last hurdle we need to clear is that which is presented by fear. "Unlearning" demands that we do more than rewiring our brains. We have to use new knowledge to face and overcome our fears. I am not naïve enough to think that this is your first time making resolutions and vowing that you will do better this time around. Still, fear remains a present reality.

According to psychiatric studies, there are nearly 2,000 classified forms of phobias. A phobia is an overwhelming, persistent, and unreasonable debilitating fear of an object or situation that poses little risk

---

[58] Fission is the process of splitting into two parts.

to the average person. By its very nature, phobia is irrational, but no less debilitating to the person feeling it.

Fears run the gamut with everything from triskaidekaphobia (the fear of the number 13) to anuptaphobia (the fear of staying single). There is even the fear of acquiring a phobia. Phobias are the most prominent mental health issue in the United States. Women reportedly have more phobias than men. Men, however, are less likely to admit they have fears, so this statistic is a bit flawed. Phobias have gotten some serious attention with the recent studies in agoraphobia, which is the fear of leaving a safe place.

What is interesting in all this is that psychiatrists insist that we are born with only two innate fears: ***Ligyrophobia*** (the fear of loud noises) and ***Basophobia*** (the fear of falling). That means all other fears are learned. Conversely, that means every other fear can be unlearned.

It is safe to say that most of us are shaped, for better or for worse, by a handful of experiences. Those defining moments can plant a seed of powerlessness, a seed of fear or a seed of faith. What hinders us in our quest for greatness is our difficulty in believing that we have a destiny to fulfill, a great purpose bequeathed to us, rooted in the very core of our being. We just can't see it. We can't help but believe that such things are left to an elite group—the most select few that God picked out of the masses to have a special role in unique times and events.

Courage is putting yourself in a defenseless position. That is what Daniel did when he went down in the lion's den. That is what Benaiah did when he chased a lion into a pit on a snowy day. That is what Esther did by defying royal protocol.

It is one thing to set a course and follow it, but it is another and quite different altogether to find your course and follow it. The essence of a life well lived is summed up in the Bible's epitaph for one of the greatest human lives ever lived, King David. The Bible simply but profoundly says, "David…served God's purpose in his own generation." (Acts 13:36) Whenever we serve God's purpose, we enter into a kairos moment that is seized by God in a way that does nothing less than change the world.

William Wilberforce was a member of the English Parliament in the late 18th century. His life was influenced by some of John Wesley's disciples, and he later became a Christian. His belief in Christ infused him with a sense of personal purpose, and he seized it with force. Wilberforce found his purpose in life sparked by his outrage over the slave trade. A most barbaric practice, slavery herded Africans into slave ships and packed them like cargo to be carried off to Western Hemisphere. Many died en route. On sugarcane and cotton plantations, African slaves were treated worse than beasts of burden. They worked on their masters' fields from can to can't, that is, from when they could tell the difference between weeds and plants until they couldn't.

Sacrificing an opportunity to become the British Prime Minister, Wilberforce instead challenged the political powers of his day to end the slave trade. His campaign began in 1787. Year after year, his efforts were defeated in Parliament, but he pressed on. He never despaired and never counted the odds against him because he had found his life's purpose. Finally, after a 20-year struggle, a majority voted in the House of Commons to end the despicable practice of the slave trade. Twenty-five years later, when Wilberforce was lying on his deathbed, slavery itself had died throughout the British Empire.

Compare this with the confession of Martin Niemoller, the German pastor who initially sent a telegram to Hitler congratulating him on his rise to power:

> *"In Germany, they came first for the communists, and I didn't speak up because I wasn't a communist. Then they came for the Jews, and I didn't speak up because I wasn't a Jew. Then they came for the trade unionists, and I didn't speak up because I wasn't a trade unionist. Then they came for the Catholics, and I didn't speak up because I was a Protestant. Then they came for me, and by this time, no one was left to speak up."*[59]

Both men had life *"defining moments"* right before them. One took the less traveled path of fearless resistance, the other chose conformity.

Few would not choose such a heroic life. What hinders us is fear, the fear of failure perhaps. However, this says more about the way we see things than it does about what is truly out there to be seen. Jesus went

---

[59] Rose, Norman, Churchill: The Unruly Giant (New York: The Free Press, 1994), p. 2.

out of his way to expand people's perspective—not only about the Kingdom of God, but also about the potential God had placed in them. "You are tied down to the mundane," Jesus once said. "I am in touch with what is beyond your horizons. You live in terms of what you see and touch. I am living on other terms. I told you that you were missing God in all this. You are at a dead end…You are missing God in your lives." (John 8:23-24 MSG)

You were given a life because God had a destiny for you individually. You are not an accident. God willed you into existence. He has not only given you life, but He also has invested you with purpose and potential. Within you is the opportunity to join with God in fulfilling the great adventure birthed in His mind for you from eternity.

God willed you into existence. He has not only given you life, but he also has invested you with purpose and potential. Within you is the opportunity to join with God in fulfilling the great adventure birthed in His mind for you from eternity.

Such has been the life of Bishop Desmond Tutu. As a Nobel Peace Prize winner known for his struggle against apartheid, he shared intimate details of fears in the dark night of his brave struggle in the effort to topple the immoral, racist, white supremacist laws. In his book, God Has a Dream, he wrote:

> *"Of course, there were times when you had to whistle in the dark to keep your morale up, and you wanted to whisper in God's ear, 'God we know you are in charge, but can't you make it a little more obvious?'"*[60]

And God did make it a little more obvious for Bishop Tutu. While sitting quietly in the garden in the dead of winter, he saw a large wooden cross without a corpse, but it had protruding nails and a crown of thorns. It was a stark reminder of his Christian faith. He noticed the grass was dead, pale and dry. No one would believe that in a few weeks, the fields would be lush, green and beautiful again. Likewise, the trees with gnarled, leafless branches would burst forth with the sap flowing so that birds would sit chirping on the leafy branches.

---

[60] Tutu, Desmond, God Has a Dream: A Vision of Hope for Our Time (New York: Doubleday, 2004), p. 3.

From this lesson of nature, the bishop was reminded that the principle of transfiguration says that nothing, no one, and no situation is "untransfigurable."[61]

> *Sometimes our humility is really timidity, as we hide our gifts or shrink from the boldness that a situation requires*
>
> *Bishop Tutu*

Following your life's purpose demands wholesale abandon, risk, sacrifice, and radical trust in the loving heart of the living God. It calls us to swim out from the shore of the known to explore the unknown without leaving anything for the swim back. This is the fearless swim to greatness.

Faith Allergies

People who fulfill their life's purpose experience the same fears as everyone else. I bet you anything Benaiah was afraid of the boogey man as a kid. We had our version of boogey man in Kitui; we called him Walola. However, like Benaiah, lion chasers have learned to stare

[61] Ibid, p. 4

down their fears. They have unlearned the fear of uncertainty, the fear of risk, the fear of looking foolish, and the countless other fears that would have otherwise held them back. They don't necessarily know more than others, but they have unlearned the fears that kept them captive. And they did it all the same way, by chasing their fears rather than running away from them. They exposed themselves to the very thing they feared most.

The disciples went back to Jerusalem, where they had all denied Christ. Abraham led his son to Mount Moriah and placed him on the altar. Moses went back to Pharaoh after 40 years of running away as a fugitive—wanted for murder. Jesus went into the wilderness for 40 days to be tested.

Is there a place of failure and shame in your past where, like the disciples, you need to return to so you may be infused with God's power? Is there an Isaac you need to lay on the altar of sacrifice? Is there a Pharaoh you need to face? Or maybe God is leading you out to give you a wilderness experience.

Every year, just before winter begins, I get a flu shot. Why? Flu season is right on us. The solution for allergies is not to run away from them. You can't. You can't avoid them. The cure is actually exposing yourself to them in small doses so you gain a greater tolerance for them. Here is the point: The cure for fear of failure is not success. It is failure. The cure for fear of rejection is not acceptance. It is rejection. The cure for loneliness is not company. It is being alone. You have got to be exposed to small quantities of whatever it is that you fear; that is how you build immunity.

Finish

In the 1986, almost 20,000 runners entered the New York City Marathon. The person who finished dead last was a man named Bob Wieland. It took Bob four days, two hours, 48 minutes, and 17 seconds to cross the finish line. It was the slowest marathon time recorded in history. Running on only his arms, Bob completed the race, which is all what mattered.

In Vietnam, 17 years earlier, Bob had lost his legs in battle. To run, Bob had to cover his fists with pads and run with his arms. He averaged about one mile an hour. When he entered the race, he already knew that the real challenge was not how fast he could run or the setbacks along the way. The real challenge was whether he had what it took to complete the race.[62] Determine today that you are going to complete your race, even if that means crawling on your hands. Determine not to quit on life regardless of the odds you face.

[62] Adopted from Steven J. Lawson, Men who win (Colorado Springs, Col. NavPress, 1992), p. 156

We can succeed in pressing on if we take hold of three essentials: First, remember those who went before you and set the pace. Second, get rid of anything that weighs you down or trips you up; you may want to start with staring down your fears. Third, make a fresh start with God and stay the course. Don't quit because of your limitations or the odds. Win in spite of them.

CPSIA information can be obtained at www.ICGtesting.com
Printed in the USA
LVOW100631200313

325082LV00002B/2/P

9 780988 766808